Bloom Before You're Planted

Gardening Tools for a Woman's Soul

Lizabeth Duckworth

Bloom Before You're Planted

Gardening Tools for a Woman's Soul

 LIFE JOURNEY®

Bringing Home the Message for Life

COOK COMMUNICATIONS MINISTRIES
Colorado Springs, Colorado • Paris, Ontario
KINGSWAY COMMUNICATIONS LTD
Eastbourne, England

Life Journey® is an imprint of
Cook Communications Ministries, Colorado Springs, CO 80918
Cook Communications, Paris, Ontario
Kingsway Communications, Eastbourne, England

BLOOM BEFORE YOU'RE PLANTED

The Web addresses (URLs) recommended throughout this book are
solely offered as a resource to the reader. The citation of these Web sites
does not in any way imply an endorsement on the part of the author or
the publisher, nor does the author or publisher vouch for their content
for the life of this book.

The poem by Carol Boyle and all personal correspondence are used by
permission of the author.

Cover Photo: Caroline Schiff/Getty Images
Cover Design: Zoë Tennesen Eck Design

First printing, 2007
Printed in the United States of America

1 2 3 4 5 6 7 8 9 10

All Scripture quotations, unless otherwise noted, are taken from the
Holy Bible, New International Version®. NIV®. Copyright © 1973, 1978,
1984 by International Bible Society. Used by permission of Zondervan.
All rights reserved. Scripture quotations marked NASB are taken from the
New American Standard Bible, © Copyright 1960, 1995 by The
Lockman Foundation. Used by permission.

ISBN 978-0-7814-4413-2
LCCN 2006932305

To Sheila Zinke,
who blooms in the lives of all around her

Contents

Acknowledgments

My heartfelt thanks to those who in some way contributed to this book: Mike Nappa, Karen Llewellyn, Charmaine Bridgens, Marion Duckworth, Lisa Barnes, Nancy Brummett, Camille Kolcz, Carol Boyle, Sara Doyle, Doris McCraw, Ben Schwenk, Jane Ambrose Morton, and Afton Rorvik.

The gardener nurtured vines
along the cemetery wall
and whistled at all times
a happy, birdlike call

she blew that happy fife
in a place of sorrow granted
'cause she'd learned the key to life
is to bloom before you're planted!

—AUTHOR UNKNOWN

Bloom Before You're Planted

The fruit of the Spirit is love, joy, peace, patience, kindness, goodness, faithfulness, gentleness and self-control. Against such things there is no law.
—GALATIANS 5:22–23

It's 5:45 a.m., and Betty's alarm couldn't be more insistent. At a pitch only a high-tech instrument of torture can deliver, it commands her to "rise and shine." Rising—but not shining—Betty launches into her day.

She makes her coffee. She wakes her kids and takes their breakfast orders. She toasts the bagel and nukes the oatmeal, sets out the juice and vitamins. After rousting the kids again, she fetches the morning paper, packs school lunches, throws on clothes, rearranges her bed-head hair, and organizes the kids out the door, into the car, and off to school. Next it's home to feed the pets, administer asthma medication (to one chronically ill cat), and finally, to dress, groom, and dive into a full day's work. She feels like she's already lived an entire day and it's only 8:15 in the morning.

The fruit of the Spirit ... is not a list of things you do.

Do you know Betty? She's me. She just might be you, too, in a slightly different outfit, with a slightly different routine. Like most modern women in our over-taxed, under-rested, pressure-filled, achievement-oriented world, Betty is busy. And the last thing she needs, you need, or I need is another to-do list. Her calendar is crammed; her Day-Timer has run out of time; her Blackberry is bursting. Hand her a book on the fruit of the Spirit and she might just smack you over the head with it ... before rushing off to her next assignment.

Not Another To-Do List

I have good news. This journey through the nine characteristics that comprise the fruit of the Spirit is not a type of spiritual must-do list at all. Instead it's a bountiful treasure: a nourishing taste of life and health, replete with benefits, just like a perfect red strawberry which promises delicious sweetness, cancer-fighting phytochemicals, vitamin C, and fiber, all wrapped up in a heart-shaped crimson package topped with a green bow.

As you progress through these pages, you'll come to discover that the fruit of the Spirit—otherwise known as love, joy, peace, patience, kindness, goodness, faithfulness, gentleness, self-control—is not a list of things you do. It's not even a pile of character traits to develop and improve upon. The fruit of the Spirit is the outgrowth of a life lived in the Spirit, a relationship with the One who wants to give you the most abundant life you can possibly have, now and into eternity.

Growing up in the southeast Denver area, which has poor soil and fickle weather, I didn't see much fruit growing in its natural state. Mom tried growing a pear tree once. I remember she sent me running into a hailstorm wearing an army blanket for protection while tenting the tiny tree with my outstretched arms to save its tender blossoms. We never ate a pear

Our connection with the Holy Spirit determines that perfect climate and environment which produces good fruit.

from that tree. Mom tried raspberry bushes too; I enjoyed the bounty of that entire harvest in a single little bowl.

The growth of good fruit in our lives is an ongoing process.

The berries were fresh, but tart. And then there were the apples shuttled in cardboard boxes from my grandparents' ranch on the eastern Colorado plains. It took a whole box to get enough apples for one pie, once you cut around all the worms and bad spots. Grandma and Grandpa didn't believe in spraying those poor, beleaguered trees. The fruit was all natural, but not plentiful, and certainly not beautiful to see.

Then I went to college in McMinnville, Oregon, deep in the heart of well-watered Willamette Valley. The soil was rich, the climate perfect for fruit-growing. Pears fell off laden trees all around us as we met outside for class one late-summer day. I walked along the little creek bed behind my dormitory and picked a bag full of the sweetest, deep purple Marionberries I'd ever tasted. After marrying, I lived in Oregon for six more years. Each summer I made time to head out to "u-pick" fields to fill boxes and bags with incredible strawberries and succulent blueberries. I'd never before experienced such agricultural adventures.

Now, there's no disrespect intended. Please don't

think my comparison of Colorado and Oregon implies that Colorado can't produce good fruit. But it clearly takes the right conditions to grow the *best* fruit. Though southwestern Colorado's Rocky Ford is famous for its cantaloupe, and Colorado's western slope does have the perfect soil and right rainfall to give us Grand Junction peaches beyond compare, it was in Oregon that I finally found fresh, sweet fruit at my fingertips, a revelation of abundance, ready for eating. The climate there was perfect for produce.

There's nothing like produce picked fresh from a tree or vine well-tended and nurtured by capable hands. The secret is in the soil, the weather, and the farmer who provides just the tending required so the fruit has no choice but to bloom and grow as its Creator designed. Isn't it interesting that a tree doesn't have to make a huge, personal effort to birth its fruit? There's no moaning or groaning or pushing (or screaming at the husband) as in human childbirth. When the tree is in its proper place, the fruit follows the blossoms as naturally as sunrise follows night. God planned it that way.

It's All about the Environment

Our connection with the Holy Spirit determines that perfect climate and environment which produces good fruit within our own lives. We can't bear fruit without him. Trying to do so would be akin to a dead vine straining to pop out a handful of juicy grapes. It won't happen without the life provided by attachment to the main Vine and its root.

A note for Galatians 5:22–26 in the *Quest Study Bible* describes it this way: "The Fruit of the Spirit is something only the Holy Spirit can produce in the life of a believer. As such, it's something we receive by faith—a gift given when we accept Christ as our Savior. At the same time, as we live in obedience to God's commands, the fruit grows and develops in our lives."

> *Bearing fruit isn't about trying; it's about yielding.*

The growth of good fruit in our lives is an ongoing process as we seek to attain spiritual maturity—a lifelong challenge. It doesn't happen all at once, and it doesn't ever stop unless we allow it to.

What does this look like? A virtual flood, according to this promise we can read in Romans 15:13: "May the God of hope fill you with all joy and peace as you trust in him, so that you may overflow with hope by the power of the Holy Spirit."

One of the functions of the Spirit is to mold your life to conform with God's, so that you reflect to the world his love, joy, peace, patience, kindness, goodness, faithfulness, gentleness, and self-control. With the

Spirit indwelling you, you find that bearing fruit isn't about trying; it's about yielding.

Isn't it ironic that the word *yield* can be used to describe the outcome of a harvest as well as the act of giving up our rights? We see a tree which *yields* a ripe crop of apples, and we *yield* the right of way to other cars (unless we're driving in Colorado Springs, where nobody yields, ever). In the chapters to come, we'll explore each individual aspect of the fruit of the Spirit, and find out how yielding to our Lord in daily life enables each of us to become ever more fruitful as the Spirit fills us continuously.

The great theological writer Charles Ryrie puts it so much more intelligently than I can. He states, "If filling relates to the control of the Spirit in one's life ... then filling is related to yieldedness. When I am willing to allow the Spirit to do what He wishes, it is up to Him to do or not to do with me whatever is His pleasure. I can check my willingness but I cannot manipulate His activities."

So we desire to bear fruit as the Holy Spirit fills us, and our goal is to yield to God as King, bowing down to him day by day, hour by hour, in every part of our beings. That sounds nice. But what does that really look like in the midst of your busy-Betty life? How do you keep that wonderful desire from becoming just another checked-off item on your ever-demanding to-do list? Take a deep breath. Remember Jesus loves you deeply and wants only the best for you. Decide to begin a journey that will last a lifetime, a journey to become more like him. Don't wait until it's too late. Bloom before you're planted.

Where should we begin? Well, what's the very first fruit on the Top Nine List detailed in Galatians 5:22–23?

It's *love*.

Might as well get ready for it, Miss Betty. Because Love is ready for you.

Chapter 1

The Fruit of the Spirit Is ... *Love*

o you enjoy a good romance? If so, I've got a tender love story for you—a true story about what it means to give your love to another person, then watch it circle around and flow out to others.

They met in New York City, nearly sixty years ago. Marion, now my mother-in-law but then a young girl, was captivated by John, a handsome, struggling actor with a giving heart. They married and soon had their first child, a son. But something was missing in the midst of their hectic, starting-out lives. They hadn't yet met Jesus Christ.

A small church in the big city proved the catalyst for a new relationship for the young family. Knowing Jesus turned their world upside down, so much so that they packed up their lives and moved across the country to plant new churches and share God's love.

Life wasn't perfect. Some dreams died while others were born and blossomed. There was never much money for the family as John and Marion worked to serve God and raise their three boys. But they made a place for me, too, in their hearts and lives when I became engaged to their eldest son in 1974. I saw the ups and downs they endured as a couple, taking each financial and life challenge one at a time, modeling faithfulness and joy in the little things: a weekend anniversary trip to the Oregon coast, two-for-one burgers at McDonald's, a carton of small wrapped packages—called a "surprise box"—bestowed on each family member for every birthday. They lived in the same little house in Salem, Oregon, for thirty years, and I couldn't envision that ever changing.

Until John had a stroke. Over the months, he grew gradually weaker while Marion struggled to be his full-time caretaker. A frequently published writer and beloved speaker, she gave up her creative time and wider ministry to minister on a much smaller scale, with long days devoted to John's medical needs and personal comforts.

Years went by and the couple at last left their small home to live with son Mark and his wife, Debbie. By that time, dementia had taken most of John's memory and mental function. The stroke stole his physical strength and control. But Marion was his loving, tender, primary nurse and caretaker right up until the end, almost one year ago.

The strain must have been nearly unbearable, yet I never heard Marion complain. She spoke honestly about how hard it was, but found that time and again, the Lord renewed her capacity to give. And she never stopped loving the man she'd shared her life with, even though he changed radically over time. Recently, Marion sent her close friends and family this poignant letter about her feelings as she marked that difficult, first wedding anniversary without her life-mate.

> *The flow of water appears nearly effortless in its constant motion.*

Yesterday was John and my fifty-seventh wedding anniversary. For the first time, we were separated.

Always we were together on our day; always we celebrated—often on the Oregon coast. Once, perhaps twenty years ago, we were almost apart. John was pastoring a new church in another state; I was nursing two ill sons at home in Oregon. Late in the day, he showed up at the door. Since one son was recuperating in our bed, I spent the night on the sofa and John on the floor beside me. We held hands and talked one another to sleep.

How would I celebrate the first anniversary in 57 years that we were apart? This time he wouldn't show up at my door with a big smile as my gift.

When I prayed, God gently reminded me of the boxes of photos and memento albums I had on the closet shelf. "Revisit your lives together." I reread my written accounts of previous anniversary celebrations, grateful that I'd taken the time to record where we went, what we ate and did. I listened to the Good Friday concert tape he recorded and one of his sermons and cried.

Before I prayed about what to do on January 2, I had decided to go to Portland where I could distract myself for the day. Instead, God led me to immerse myself in our years together. How glad I am that I listened! For, as a result, I have greater peace—especially about the periods of chaos in our lives. Here's how I expressed my thoughts about that in a letter I wrote to John on my sixtieth birthday: "Going through the tangles with someone you love and who loves you is the best of all ways to make the trip." That statement is true now more than ever.

The agape love that John introduced into my life is the greatest anniversary gift anyone could have.... Before I met John, I felt unloved. Here was a man who excelled in agape. Sometimes he rejected my ideas, but never me. The years bathed in that kind of acceptance prepared me for the absolute love of God that finally made me whole.

For the rest of my life on earth, I want to help others through the tangles in their lives and love them forward.

Blessings,
Marion

In so many ways, both Marion and John evidenced the fruit of the Spirit, especially the love that comes from God and goes forth as a result of the Spirit residing in willing hearts. And the love and acceptance Marion found in her husband of fifty-six years circles around and continues to flow out to others as she serves them sacrificially. It is an everlasting cycle of receiving and giving.

A Waterwheel of Love

The love exemplified in both Marion and John's marriage and their lives reminds me of the old wooden waterwheel off Interstate 70 in the mountain town of Idaho Springs, Colorado. The ingenious device resembles a large, wooden Ferris wheel, except instead of carrying happy people, it carries ice-cold water. The river's flow turns the wheel and fills its troughs, which are then lifted up and around. Gravity empties the water into a new channel. The flow—which was once used to power equipment before easy electricity could do the same job—works continuously and appears nearly effortless in its constant motion.

In the same way, the love of God flows into our lives, filling us and then spilling out in new directions, refreshing and powering the world around us—if we let it. We don't need to work at it with strain and effort. We just need to yield.

Here's another example of waterwheel love: a tiny, impoverished, powerless nun who rose to prominence because of her overflowing love and the way it changed lives and hearts—Mother Teresa of Calcutta.

Years ago British author and filmmaker Malcolm Muggeridge visited Mother Teresa and her Mission of Charity and described their lives in his book *Something Beautiful for God.*

> Their lives are tough and austere by worldly standards, certainly; yet, I never met such delightful, happy women, or such an atmosphere of joy as they create. Mother Teresa, as she is fond of explaining, attaches the utmost importance to their joyousness. The poor, she says, deserve not just service and dedication, but also the joy that belongs to human love. This is what the Sisters give them abundantly.
>
> But Mother Teresa and her helpers do not give this love or project their joy through their own human efforts. Their expressions of love and joy are the outpouring of hearts filled with the love of God. She said, "'Thou shalt love the Lord thy God with thy whole heart, with thy whole soul and with thy whole mind.' This is the commandment of the great God, and He cannot command the impossible. Love is a fruit in season at all times, and within reach of every hand. Anyone may gather it and no limit is set. Everyone can reach this love through meditation, spirit of prayer and sacrifice, by an intense inner life."

Mother Teresa's list of tools by which to gather the "fruit of love" was her own recipe for intimacy with God, the key factor in having an abundance of love to give, and something you'll be encouraged to explore in detail later in this chapter. For now, with a little imagination, let's look into the life of One who knew God better than any other. Jesus Christ modeled intimacy with God that was expressed through actions both loving and sacrificial.

Measuring Love by the Foot

Simon Peter is looking forward to the Passover Feast. It has been a busy day and now his body is weary; his stomach growling. The scent of roasted lamb fills the air as he reclines at last, ready to let the day's thoughts and troubles roll away in an atmosphere of friendship and learning at Jesus' side.

But what is this? Jesus suddenly stands up from the table. He removes his outer clothing, wraps a towel around his waist, and pours water into a basin. Then he moves around the room, washing his disciples' feet and drying them with the towel he has wrapped around himself.

Simon Peter glances at his own dirty feet, encrusted with the grime and grit of filthy Jerusalem streets. He sniffs and smells a stink that can only be the remnants of animal droppings. His toenails are dark and scraggly;

on his right heel a blister rears its red and weeping head. How could he let his Master even come near these disgusting feet, let alone touch them, wash them, and dry them with the very towel he is wearing?

Love each other as I have loved you.

As Jesus approaches him, Simon Peter protests, "Lord, are you going to wash my feet?"

Jesus replies, "You do not realize now what I am doing, but later you will understand."

"No," Peter argues. "You will never wash my feet." Even the suggestion is appalling; he can't allow it. He'll be humiliated in front of the One he most wants to impress.

Jesus answers gently, "Unless I wash you, you have no part with me."

No part with Jesus? That would be devastating. Simon Peter blurts out his devotion: "Then, Lord, … not just my feet but my hands and head as well!" (John 13:9).

Jesus finishes the foot-washing, puts on his clothes, and returns to his place at the meal. "Do you understand what I have done for you?" he says. "You call me 'Teacher' and 'Lord,' and rightly so, for that is what I am. Now that I, your Lord and Teacher, have washed your feet, you also should wash one another's feet. I have set you an example that you should do as I have done for you. I tell you the truth, no servant is greater than his master, nor is a messenger greater than the one who sent him. Now that you know these things, you will be blessed if you do them."

As the evening stretches on, Peter tries to absorb and memorize every word that comes from the Master's mouth. They are commands given to the troops in a tone that is strong without being harsh. Peter strains to fold the teaching into his mind as well as his heart, so that Jesus' words will echo in his soul forever.

Jesus says, As the Father has loved me, so have I loved you. Now remain in my love. If you obey my commands, you will remain in my love, just as I have obeyed my Father's commands and remain in his love.... My command is this: Love each other as I have loved you. Greater love has no one than this, that he lay down his life for his friends. You are my friends if you do what I command. I no longer call you servants, because a servant does not know his master's business. Instead, I have called you friends, for everything that I learned from my Father I have made known to you. You did not choose me, but I chose you and appointed you to go and bear fruit—fruit that will last. Then the Father will give you whatever you ask in my name. This is my command: Love each other. (John 15:9–17)

Simon Peter regards his feet, spotless for the moment thanks to Jesus' selfless demonstration of love in action. With all his being he wants to be just like his Master. But will he prove faithful when the time of testing comes? Will he be asked to lay down his life for his friends? Will he love as Jesus loves?

As Jesus teaches long into the night, Simon Peter's heart surges with feelings of love and devotion, while his mind battles pinpricks of self-doubt. He knows his weaknesses. He knows his desires. Only time will tell if he is a true disciple. (Retold from John 13:1–17; 15:9–17.)

Loving like Jesus loved ... has to be an outpouring of his love inside of us.... The key is learning to sit back and let Jesus minister to us.

Most of us can identify with Simon Peter's passion to follow Christ on one hand, and his human weaknesses on the other. We want to be like Jesus, washing the feet of others in humility and service. But in the end, like Peter, we find we can't do it without the Holy Spirit prompting us, guiding us, filling us, supporting us. Loving like Jesus loved is not a lifestyle you just decide to live out. It has to be an outpouring of his love inside of us, love that is renewed every morning.

Perhaps the key is learning to sit back and let Jesus minister to us so that we are then able to minister to others. As he washes our feet, cleans us up, and makes us presentable, we are refreshed. We are motivated by the model he demonstrates. We are enabled by him to fulfill our calling of loving service in the lives of sometimes-difficult coworkers, children, spouses, friends, and family members.

Loving others is a deliberate choice, not an outgrowth of altruistic feelings. It does result in the bloom of joy, but it is rooted in basic obedience. The authors of the Victor *Bible Knowledge Commentary* put it this way: "A believer is motivated by the wonder of Jesus' love, which is patterned after the Father's love in its quality and extent. 'Remain in My love' might seem to be mystical but Jesus makes it very concrete. Obedience to the Father's commands is the same for a disciple as it was for the Son. Active dependence and loving obedience are the proper paths for all of God's children."

So what do "active dependence and loving obedience" look like? For me, today they have taken on a very specific form. My fourteen-year-old son woke up with a fever and a cough, meaning no school for him. I had my list of to-dos—including an important meeting at church—already prepared. But my role as a mother takes first place, so I started reorganizing my schedule and changing my plans for the day. When I let a friend know the situation, she demonstrated practical love to me by calling from the grocery store to see what I needed her to pick up there. She bought two cartons of "Go-GURT" that my sick boy had requested, and dropped them off at the house. Her act of love allowed me to show love to my son as I cared for him. Meanwhile, I experienced God's love and presence as he helped me focus on writing this chapter while my Jonathan slept peacefully. The cycle of receiving and giving has been renewing my spirit all day, keeping me at peace in the midst of canceled plans and unexpected schedule changes.

Love in Action

What does love look like when it's in motion, in action? Where can we go to see a picture of that overflowing love that nourishes the lives of others? Let's turn to the Old Testament for a beautiful example of a sacrificial love that swirls full circle.

The young woman's name was Ruth, and though she was still young she had already suffered a huge loss and a broken heart. The death of her husband dashed her dreams of home and family and left her alone with her widowed mother-in-law, Naomi, and her sister-in-law, Orpah, also a widow. The three women had been dependent on their husbands for support and protection; now they had nothing except each other.

Defeated by her losses, Naomi planned to return to her homeland of Judah, leaving her daughters-in-law behind in Moab, because they belonged to the land and the people there. She told the young women, "Go back, each of you, to your mother's home. May the LORD show kindness to you, as you have shown to your dead and to me. May the LORD grant that each of you will find rest in the home of another husband."

Her kisses made them cry. They refused to let the older woman leave without them, insisting on taking the long journey to the land of Naomi's people.

May the Lord repay you for what you have done.

But Naomi said, "Return home, my daughters. Why would you come with me? Am I going to have any more sons, who could become your husbands? Return home, my daughters; I am too old to have another husband. Even if I thought there was still hope for me—even if I had a husband tonight and then gave birth to sons—would you wait until they grew up? Would you remain unmarried for them? No, my daughters. It is more bitter for me than for you, because the LORD's hand has gone out against me!"

At this they wept again. Then Orpah kissed her mother-in-law good-bye, but Ruth clung to her. "Don't urge me to leave you or to turn back from you," she said. "Where you go I will go, and where you stay I will stay. Your people will be my people and your God my God. Where you die I will die, and there I will be buried. May the LORD deal with me, be it ever so severely, if anything but death separates you and me."

Ruth's pledge of loyalty would be tested on the lengthy journey to Bethlehem in Judah and through times of hunger and uncertainty. Ruth was reduced to gleaning the leftovers from harvested barley fields in order to feed herself and Naomi. But she persevered.

Her goodness and industry did not go unrewarded. She caught the eye of Boaz, owner of the barley field where she was working. He told her, "Don't go and glean in another field and don't go away from here. Stay here with my servant girls. Watch the field where the men are harvesting and follow along after the girls. I have told the men not to touch you. And whenever you are thirsty, go and get a drink from the water jars the men have filled."

Ruth bowed down with her face to the ground. "Why have I found such favor in your eyes that you notice me—a foreigner?"

Boaz replied, "I've been told all about what you have done for your mother-in-law since the death of your husband—how you left your father and mother and your homeland and came to live with a people you did not know before. May the LORD repay you for what you have done. May you be richly rewarded by the LORD, the God of Israel, under whose wings you have come to take refuge." (Taken from Ruth 1:1–17; 2:1–13.)

Ruth was richly rewarded for her unyielding love. Boaz courted her, then married her. He protected her and her mother-in-law, Naomi, and eventually their family line produced David, the greatest king of Israel, a man after God's own heart, and author of many of the Psalms.

You can read the entire account in the book of Ruth. Better than any novel, it illustrates the power of sacrificial love as Ruth refused to take the easy, predictable path in order to enhance the lives of all around her. God filled her cup to overflowing and provided her with the strength she needed to be the woman he wanted her to be.

What about you? Do you feel like you've reached your maximum capacity for giving love to those in your stretched and busy life? Or have you recognized that when you are constantly being filled with living Water, your well of love can never run dry?

The following activities are designed to help you dig deeper and discover what "active dependence and loving obedience" might look like in your own life.

Gardener's Tools for Life

Start a "Fruit of the Spirit" journal. Let it serve as the record of your journey, your growth, your desire to *Bloom Before You're Planted!* If you like to be visual, decorate it with colorful, fruit-themed pictures that you draw yourself, cut from magazines, or find on the Internet. Make it your companion as you study the fruit of the Spirit.

If you like to be tactile (or even if you're just hungry), sit down with your journal opened on your lap and a delicious piece of fruit close at hand. Slow down and take a few minutes to savor the taste of the fruit as you contemplate the fruit of love in your life. Here are some questions and ideas that you might want to carefully think through and write about in your journal:

1. Is it hard for you to allow Jesus to wash your dirty feet? Why or why not?

2. Jesus says we are to remain in his love. How do you picture yourself doing that in the course of a typical day?

3. Are there people in your life you find hard to love? How can you show them love in spite of your feelings?

4. List things you do that help you feel close to God and filled with refreshment from his living Water. How can you make time for more of this communion on a regular basis? How might you develop the "intense inner life" described by Mother Teresa?

5. The following words describe characteristics of a perfect piece of fruit. Compare them to your relationship with God as it is now and as you'd like it to be.
    *   Sweet
    *   Nourishing
    *   Invigorating
    *   Complex
    *   Beautiful

6. In his classic book *The Fight*, John White has written that the heart "cannot be

squeezed to give forth sweetness. It needs to be heavy with the love of God, yielding its refreshment to the slightest pressure from my fellow Christians. As I find my joy in Him, so my capacity to give will exceed my need to receive." Is your heart "heavy with the love of God?" What might make it more so?

Meditate on these passages of Scripture. Revisit them each day for a week.

How great is the love the Father has lavished on us, that we should be called children of God! And that is what we are! ... This is the message you heard from the beginning: We should love one another.... Dear children, let us not love with words or tongue but with actions and in truth. This then is how we know that we belong to the truth, and how we set our hearts at rest in his presence whenever our hearts condemn us. For God is greater than our hearts, and he knows everything.

Dear friends, if our hearts do not condemn us, we have confidence before God and receive from him anything we ask, because we obey his commands and do what pleases him. And this is his command: to believe in the name of his Son, Jesus Christ, and to love one another as he commanded us. (1 John 3:1, 11, 18–23)

Love is patient, love is kind. It does not envy, it does not boast, it is not proud. It is not rude, it is not self-seeking, it is not easily angered, it keeps no record of wrongs. Love does not delight in evil but rejoices with the truth. It always protects, always trusts, always hopes, always perseveres.

Love never fails. (1 Cor. 13:4–8)

Chapter 2

The Fruit of the Spirit Is ...

Joy

There's one event each year that consistently tugs at my heart. It's not Christmas Day or Valentine's Day. It's not even my birthday or a special anniversary.

It's the first day of school. My twin boys have been in school ten years now, and the experience is always the same. I expect my feelings to get buried in the wild rush to gather up supplies, find shoes, remember sack lunches, and head out the door in a flurry of activity. I drop Chris and Jon off in front of the school and say good-bye. Then it really hits me.

Tears sting my eyes and I'm flooded with an array of emotions:

- happiness, because I know my boys will have productive, structured time, and I'll be free from stressing over them while I'm home and worrying about them while I'm gone
- wistfulness, because I see them advancing one more year, growing up before my eyes, and needing me less and less
- nostalgia, because I remember when school was simpler and it was easier to help with their problems (and their math homework)
- pride, because my kids are growing into young men who seem more than capable of standing on their own two feet

Joy is a hybrid fruit. Joy is a combination of elements that can be both bitter and sweet.

Combined, all these feelings equal joy. What is joy? In some ways, it's a hybrid fruit.

Have you read about, eaten, or seen in your local grocery store these new-fangled hybrid fruits—fruits with funny names such as "pluot" and "tangelo"? Ever wonder where they come from? Well, I'm no agricultural genius, but I'm pretty sure that as growers seek to combine the best qualities in a plum and an apricot or an orange and a tangerine, for instance, they cross breed the two fruits. And how does that work? I'm not sure, but I'm guessing it has something to do with soft music, candles, and a nice, cozy fruit basket. Romance ensues and we get pluots and tangelos.

Like hybrid fruit, joy is a combination of elements that can be both bitter and sweet. True joy is not as straightforward as basic happiness. It's a complex quality that draws on other fruit of the Spirit, such as peace, and other spiritual characteristics, such as trust and hope.

Life brings many opportunities for joy, if we will just embrace them—as did Ben and Anna, young missionaries who studied together at a language school in the Himalayan foothills. In a recent letter, they told this story:

> In early November we heard about an abandoned baby who had been left at a nearby hospital. Some friends of ours took her home when she was three days old, because the hospital could no longer care for her. Our friends, although very happy to be foster parents, were not in a good position to adopt the baby, who they named Joy. As we prayed, and many of you prayed alongside us, we felt the Lord leading us to pursue the adoption of little Joy.
>
> When she was about ten days old, we found out that she had spina bifida and needed surgery as soon as possible. God provided a good surgeon in Delhi who was willing to do the surgery for free, so we took Joy on a nine-hour car ride to the hospital. There we discovered that she also

had a severe form of congenital heart disease and would probably not live too much longer. The doctors said that surgery would be far too dangerous, so Joy's foster family took her home to care for her until she went home to be with our heavenly Father a few weeks later.

Through this situation we learned so much about trusting Christ. At times we were overwhelmed, wondering if we would be able to handle taking care of a child with major disabilities in India. Before taking Joy to the hospital for surgery, we felt that maybe it would be too much for us. At that point, we knew that God wanted us to do all we could to get help for this precious girl and to keep on trusting Him for the outcome.

In the midst of sorrow, we are thankful that she had a happy and peaceful life and did not have to go through the pain of surgery. Our Father chose to take her home and we are comforted to know that she is safe in His care now. We feel so blessed to have been a part of Joy's life on earth. She was a precious little girl whom we loved and will always remember. Thank you for your prayers through all of this.

A picture of little Joy at two weeks of age shows a beautiful, bright-eyed baby swaddled in pink and blue blankets, the sweetest expression on her face. I can see how Ben and Anna fell in love with her, and I imagine how it broke their hearts to lose her. But their trust in God brought joy out of sorrow and gives them hope to share with others. That's an example of true joy in all its complexity.

Joy in the Center
of a Busy Life

We too easily get caught up in the activities that dominate our days—whether related to our jobs, family responsibilities, church events, education, or even those few fun pastimes we choose to fill our limited free time. For some of us, that's just sleeping.

We find ourselves consumed with logistics, schedules, and piecing together a day that fits it all in and still allows us to grab a meal and do a little housecleaning, filing, pet care, laundry, bill paying, and doctor and dentist visits. And let's not forget the occasional time splurge on personal grooming: haircuts or coloring, manicures, shopping for clothes and shoes, or finding a one-step face cream that lifts, tones, de-wrinkles, eliminates acne, and protects from killer sun rays.

Nurturing joy ... will help you move through your days with assurance and serenity.

Likely, there's no line on our list for "making room to nurture joy." But there should be. Nurturing joy is a process that will help you move through your days with assurance and serenity, two qualities that can change a hectic life into a fulfilling one. We are about to explore what it means to respond to our heavenly Father in the same way Jesus did.

In human terms, it could look a bit like the kind of joy described in this e-mail from my friend Sara Doyle:

Last night, after a long and frustrating day at work, I was running late for rehearsal. I pulled into the church parking lot, jumped out of the car and made a beeline for the building, trying to make sure I had everything I needed. That's when I heard a small voice across the parking lot. I turned to find Will, my four-year-old friend, running toward me. He held out his arms to be picked up and just fell into my arms.

> *Joy ... is a reflection of your submission to and dependence on the One who made you.*

The look of pure joy on his face was amazing. It baffles me how this child can think so much of me that just seeing me makes his world complete.

The best thing is, his joy is so contagious. When I see those sparkling eyes and that bright smile, I can't help but be overwhelmed by joy as well. Seeing Will last night washed away the day's aggravations and tension and just filled me with joy.

Keep in mind that joy is fruit of the Spirit—a complex, multi-faceted jewel of a fruit. It is an outgrowth of the Holy Spirit's active work in our lives. Bountiful joy in your own world is a reflection of your submission to and dependence on the One who made you and who wants to bring out the best qualities you have to offer. Let's see how that is demonstrated in the life of Jesus, as I imagine the scene and retell it in my own words.

Under the Water and Up to the Sky

He's strange, this John the Baptist. Obviously a poor man, his camel's hair garment looks scratchy and ill-made, held together by a worn leather belt. His beard is wild, but his eyes are wilder as he pours out passion for God and a message of repentance and the coming of the Lord.

Followers crowd the banks of the Jordan river, waiting for John. Desiring to turn from their sinful ways and make a new start with God, they've clustered there to take turns going under the water. Before John appears, they hear his voice confronting religious leaders with harsh truth.

> You brood of vipers! Who warned you to flee from the coming wrath? Produce fruit in keeping with repentance.... The ax is already at the

root of the trees, and every tree that does not
produce good fruit will be cut down and thrown
into the fire. I baptize you with water for repentance. But after me will come one who is more
powerful than I, whose sandals I am not fit to
carry. He will baptize you with the Holy Spirit
and with fire. (Matt. 3:7–11)

Daily, John's compelling message continues to draw
new faces to the riverbank. One day, he recognizes a
face that emerges from the crowd; it belongs to Jesus.
When John sees his cousin, he is awash in humility. He
tries to dissuade Jesus from the act of baptism, saying,
"I need to be baptized by you, and do you come to me?"

But Jesus replies, "Let it be so now; it is proper for
us to do this to fulfill all righteousness."

John knows that Jesus is right. He reaches out his hand
to draw his cousin into the water and by his side. Down goes
Jesus, then up he rises, and at that instant, the sky itself
cracks open. The Spirit of God descends like a dove and
alights on the Son.

The key to joy is simple obedience, submission, and a heart that is humble.

The crowd is
hushed in awe, and
suddenly all hear a
voice from heaven
saying, "This is my
Son, whom I love;
with him I am well
pleased."

The face of
Jesus shines with

the pure joy of doing the Father's will. Watching, and knowing he will always remember this powerful moment, John thanks God for allowing him to play a part in it. (See Matt. 3:1–17.)

John the Baptist and others on the Jordan River shore that day witnessed a great act of willing obedience. Jesus didn't have to be baptized; that act was actually for people who needed to repent. As the sinless Son of God, Jesus had no need to repent. Nor did Jesus' baptism change his divine status; he did not become the Son of God at his baptism. But, as always, he acted out of a heart eager to please his Father.

> *You can counteract that natural tendency to put yourself first and God last.*

Some Bible scholars suggest three reasons why Jesus submitted to John's baptism:

1. To show he was in full agreement with God's overall plan
2. To identify with the nation of Israel
3. To indicate his acceptance and initiation of his messianic mission (*Bible Knowledge Commentary on the New Testament*, 105)

Jesus submitted to the will of the Father and found joy in that obedience. No doubt his baptism was a solemn occasion, but it must have also been a time to celebrate. Surely there was joy in hearing these affirming words from God the Father: "This is my Son, whom I love; with him I am well pleased."

> *Praise allows the Holy Spirit to bring forth the fruit of joy.*

Is there a picture here for us as we seek to nurture joy in our ordinary lives? And could it be that the key is simple obedience, submission, and a heart that is humble—giving God his proper place in our lives?

It Sounds like Praise

These days it isn't easy to maintain a humble heart. Our culture tells us to fight for our rights. Our minds cry out for more control. Our busy schedules keep us on the run; we jostle for the best spot as we drive our cars, stand in checkout lines, negotiate crowded aisles, and compete for higher-paying jobs. Our lives become about getting ahead, gaining space, moving along. Submission sounds like giving in, standing still, bowing down. A bit countercultural, don't you think?

But you can counteract that natural tendency to put yourself first and God last. There's a little action you can incorporate into even the busiest days, and it will help you remember who you are and who God is. It's called praise. Practicing praise allows the Holy Spirit to bring forth the fruit of joy in your life.

Many of us think of praise as a Sunday morning thing. We go to church and pray, sing some songs, maybe clap our hands or get a little more physical. But why should we limit ourselves to Sunday morning praise times that often follow an unchanging pattern? Doesn't the Lord want us to find joy in expressing our love for him in individual ways, using the gifts he has given us?

Psalm 150 (NASB) provides an inspiring description of creative praise. Verse 1 tells us *where* to praise God. "Praise God in His sanctuary." When you see "sanctuary," do you get a mental image of your church's sanctuary or auditorium? I do.

But the verse also tells us to praise God "in His mighty expanse"—that is, in all the world, from our inmost beings to the heights of the heavens. So just because you're outside walking the dog or inside scrubbing the bathtub, don't feel you aren't in a position to praise.

"Praise Him for His mighty deeds; praise Him according to His excellent greatness" (v. 2). Here the psalmist describes *what* we should praise God for. We need to thank him not only for what he has done for us lately, but also for his very nature.

In church or at my set prayer times I sometimes find myself focusing on God's "mighty deeds." I praise him for the food on my table, the roof over my head, my family, and my life. But in spontaneous acts of praise I tend to acknowledge God's greatness and goodness. When I recognize his power and love, I gain new confidence that he'll continue to meet my needs each day. And that leads me down the path of pure joy.

Is joy possible when facing trouble?

How are we to praise God? "With trumpet sound ... with harp and lyre ... with timbrel and dancing ... with stringed instruments and pipe ... with loud cymbals" (vv. 3–5). Here we see a whole gamut of instruments that could be used to praise God. And not only music, but all the arts can be used for God's glory.

Verse 6 describes *who* should praise God: "Everything that has breath." We'll have to wait until heaven to be part of such a universal praise song. Meanwhile, we can praise the Lord as long as we ourselves have breath.

Joy in the Difficult Times

What happens when we find ourselves in the middle of intense stress, even terribly painful days that follow loss and deep disappointment? Where is the fruit of joy during those periods of life? Is joy *possible* when facing trouble?

Contemplate these words from the book of James: "Consider it pure joy, my brothers, whenever you face trials of many kinds, because you know that the testing of your faith develops perseverance. Perseverance must finish its work so that you may be mature and complete, not lacking anything. If any of you lacks wisdom, he should ask God, who gives generously to all without finding fault, and it will be given to him. But when he asks, he must believe and not doubt, because he who doubts is like a wave of the sea, blown and tossed by the wind" (1:2–6).

Does this mean we should derive pleasure from pain? Not at all. James is describing a unique kind of joy—the deep sense of well-being that comes from knowing

> *Joy is not a happy feeling; it's a decision to depend on God.*

that God is in control of everything in our lives. It's an assurance that he is constantly at work, using the events in our lives to bear fruit of endurance and patience.

It is crucial to distinguish joy from happiness. Real joy can be ours even in the least happy times. It's not a happy feeling; it's a decision to depend on God for the outcome of every life occurrence.

I experienced this when, after many years of infertility and three miscarriages, I at last gave birth to my first child, Katherine Ann. My dreams of motherhood instantly shattered when I learned that her low birthweight and inability to breathe on her own were the result of a rare birth defect, Trisomy 18. She lived only one week, but in that week she gave to my husband and me the fulfillment of our wish to be parents—all the joys and pain of loving a child, condensed into seven brief days.

I didn't feel happy; in fact, I cried many tears of grief and loss. But in time I came to see how God brought forth good fruit. This fruit stemmed from the way my husband and I responded in joy to Katherine's part in our lives. People were encouraged and many heard the message of the gospel at Katherine's memorial services. Others found renewed faith.

Because she touched so many lives while on earth, I try not to think of her with sadness, but rather with joy. I know she is in heaven, and I trust that God will unite us some day and we'll find infinite joy together in his presence.

Joy in Action

The picture of joy in action isn't always one of a smiling face or hands uplifted. It could look more like tear-filled eyes cast toward heaven and trusting God for comfort. Yet sometimes joy in action looks like pure praise, even like happy feet. Miriam, the sister of Moses, gives us an unforgettable Old Testament moment of joy.

The bold march of the Israelites away from Egypt had turned into a foot race. Miriam, along with her brothers, Moses and Aaron, were leading the people away from slavery and toward a new beginning, when they found themselves hotly pursued by the soldiers of Egypt.

As Pharaoh approached, the Israelites looked up, and there were the Egyptians, marching after them. They were terrified and cried out to the Lord. They said to Moses, "Was it because there were no graves in Egypt that you brought us to the desert to die? What have you done to us by bringing us out of Egypt?... It would have been better for us to serve the Egyptians than to die in the desert!"

Moses answered the people, "Do not be afraid. Stand firm and you will see the deliverance the LORD will bring you today. The Egyptians you see today you will never see again. The LORD will fight for you; you need only to be still" (Ex. 14:10–14).

Then Moses heard the voice of the Lord and followed the instructions. He stretched out his hand and everyone rushed ahead on dry land as sea waters stood at attention on either side. Miriam and the others hurried through the passageway, just ahead of chariots and armed Egyptians.

As she looked back, Miriam could see a pillar of fire and cloud, and the Egyptian army in chaos, with wheels flying off chariots and horses mired in the mud. She turned away and rushed ahead to the Red Sea's shore, hurrying toward the crowd there on dry ground.

Again Moses stretched out his hand and the waters flowed over their pursuers, covering the chariots and horsemen entirely. The Israelites were now safe on the far shore, saved by the power of the Lord.

In gratitude and rejoicing, Miriam took her tambourine in hand and led the women in a song and dance of praise: "Sing to the LORD, for he is highly exalted. The horse and its rider he has hurled into the sea" (Ex. 15:21).

As all Israel joined their voices in a song to the Lord, they recounted his amazing feats and praised his power:

> The LORD is my strength and my song;
>   he has become my salvation.
> He is my God, and I will praise him,
>   my father's God, and I will exalt him....
> Who among the gods is like you, O LORD?
>   Who is like you—
>   majestic in holiness,
>   awesome in glory,
>   working wonders?
> You stretched out your right hand
>   and the earth swallowed them.
> In your unfailing love you will lead
>   the people you have redeemed.
> In your strength you will guide them
>   to your holy dwelling....
> You will bring them in and plant them
>   on the mountain of your inheritance—
>   the place, O LORD, you made for your
>   dwelling,

the sanctuary, O LORD, your hands
established.
The LORD will reign
forever and ever.
(Ex. 15:2, 11–13, 17–18)

Read the entire account in Exodus 11—15 to more fully understand and appreciate Miriam's and the Israelites' incredible joy at their deliverance out of bondage in Egypt. Their goals of freedom and a new life seemed unattainable, but the Lord had his own plans for them.

He has plans for you as well. Look back in your personal history to see how he has cleared pathways in your life and helped you overcome seemingly insurmountable obstacles. When you give him credit for all the good in your life, your joy in the present will grow accordingly.

Gardener's Tools for Life

Do you want to nurture joy in your life? Practice incorporating the sacrifice of praise into your daily life. Trust me. It won't feel like a sacrifice at all.

After all, our forms of praise are unlimited. We can dedicate our lives as hymns to God if we apply the words of Paul: "Whatever you do in word or deed, do all in the name of the Lord Jesus, giving thanks through Him to God the Father" (Col. 3:17 NASB).

Has God gifted you with the ability to create beauty? Praise him in the crafts you make, in the home you decorate, in the flowers you plant and care for.

Relationships with family and friends are opportunities to praise God by expressing love in concrete ways. Write in your journal about a plan to surprise somebody with a loving act this week.

You can praise God in your work, doing it to the best of your ability with a joyful heart.

You can praise him in your day-to-day chores. Do you have to water the plants? Instead of talking to them (some people claim it makes them grow better), talk to God. Thank him for what he is doing to help you grow spiritually.

When you bake a cake, play an instrument, or write in your journal, keep an attitude of praise. Be open to the wealth of opportunities God gives you daily to praise in all ways!

Meditate on these passages of Scripture. Revisit them each day for a week:

Praise the LORD.
How good it is to sing praises to our God,
> how pleasant and fitting to praise him!

The LORD builds up Jerusalem;
> he gathers the exiles of Israel.

He heals the brokenhearted
> and binds up their wounds.

He determines the number of the stars
> and calls them each by name.

Great is our Lord and mighty in power;
> his understanding has no limit.

The LORD sustains the humble
> but casts the wicked to the ground.

Sing to the LORD with thanksgiving;
> make music to our God on the harp.

He covers the sky with clouds;
> he supplies the earth with rain
> and makes grass grow on the hills.

He provides food for the cattle
> and for the young ravens when they call.

His pleasure is not in the strength of the horse,
> nor his delight in the legs of a man;
>> the LORD delights in those who fear him,
> who put their hope in his unfailing love.

(Ps. 147:1–11)

Praise be to the LORD,
> for he has heard my cry for mercy.

The LORD is my strength and my shield;
> my heart trusts in him, and I am helped.

My heart leaps for joy
> and I will give thanks to him in song.

(Ps. 28:6–7)

Many are asking, "Who can show us any
    good?"
  Let the light of your face shine upon us,
    O LORD.
You have filled my heart with greater joy
    than when their grain and new wine abound.
    (Ps. 4:6–7)

Chapter 3

The Fruit of the Spirit Is ... *Peace*

I n my young-married, pre-kids days, I kept (by choice) a busy schedule. Between work, volunteer activities at church, exercise appointments with friends, and creative projects with my husband, I was always on the go. At times, life seemed stressful. A few piles of unfiled papers on my corner desk meant my house was messy. Sloppy frosting on the Christmas cookies I made to bring to work threw me into an identity crisis. I struggled to keep up with my correspondence, and felt like a bad person if I owed Grandma or my friend Leslie a letter for more than a few weeks.

Then I was handed a small clue about the way other women struggled with less peaceful lives. My friend Sandy dropped by my house. She worked outside the home, was a mother of four high-action kids, and superintended a large, often chaotic household complete with dogs and a screaming macaw. We started to talk about a project she needed help on, when she suddenly stopped midsentence. She paused for a few moments, took a deep breath, and said, "It's so peaceful here." I laughed, because I didn't understand the contrast between my barely lived-in home and her very lived-in life.

The kind of soul-deep peace I long for is often an elusive dream.

Now in my hyperactive, new-millennium days of trying to mother twin teenagers, work several part-time jobs, write a book, be a wife, keep up with fast-paced technology, and get the family's dinner on the table, my peace is consistently shattered. Unfiled papers have morphed into a house cluttered with the dregs of schoolwork and half-started science projects. Christmas cookies for anybody have crumbled into a sweet memory. And I haven't written a real letter in years, letting backed-up e-mail at home and work serve as my life's guilt-monger and self-esteem basher.

The kind of soul-deep peace I long for is often an elusive dream, not just for me but for many friends in various stages of life.

I know young mothers who spend their days chasing toddlers, feeding and changing babies, and longing for a nap but instead folding laundry while the baby sleeps. I see women at work, both single and married, with or without kids, looking completely cool and composed in skirted suits and heels, but inside feeling desperate to keep up with growing workloads in departments that continue to be downsized. Myself, I'm becoming one of a vast platoon of mothers who schedule their lives around teenagers who still need rides to school, practices, part-time jobs, or their four-hundred-house weekly newspaper route.

A few years ago, while working full time, my need for peace was symbolized by the long counter that divides kitchen space from the family room in my house. That counter was a magnet for piles of papers, free-floating projects, leftover Legos, and every other piece of clutter we owned. Sometimes I'd come out of my denial and actually look at it, wistfully dreaming of a day when life would calm down and I could clear that counter.

That day finally came, but only because I was sidelined by a battle with breast cancer. The kitchen counter first filled with flower arrangements from well-wishers, and when those wilted and got tossed, I at last had time to keep it cleaned off. My days of recovery and a slower pace helped me reclaim the counter space, but real life has resumed, and today I see the piles beginning to grow once again. If the counter represents my inner life and the peace of the Spirit, then I can see I should continue to make changes. It's not a good idea to postpone bearing the fruit of peace until a health crisis forces change.

What about you? If a kitchen counter represented the state of your soul, would yours be overflowing with junk, or would it be cleared of all but a beautiful vase of flowers?

Maybe peace looks like something else in your own life. Take a moment to picture what that might be. A place in the yard to sit in the shade? A cozy chair and a cup of tea? A circle of quiet where you can hear yourself breathe or even think?

My friend Sara recently e-mailed me this lovely piece about peace in the midst of her sometimes-hectic life:

> I finished the test about an hour ago. As I walked away from the classroom, I started to panic. Despite my checking and rereading of my essays, I just knew I missed something major; that I had misread the questions; that something had gone wrong. I felt that my six months of preparing had come to nothing and I just knew I had failed.
>
> My eyes focused on the sidewalk in front of me as I headed for my car. I even started thinking about how I would have to retake the test in three short months. Just as my eyes welled up with tears at my failure, a butterfly fluttered across my path. I watched it as it danced in front of me. I thought of the day before when I had been studying, and I had seen a butterfly then as well. That sight calmed me. I felt a peace come over me, an assurance that everything would be fine.

> I still don't know if I passed the test or not,
> but I now know that whatever the outcome, every-
> thing will be okay. So, I'll be waiting to hear my
> results and whatever comes, I'm okay with it.

As you hold onto your own mind's picture of peace on earth, let's consider what peace looked like when Jesus spent time with his friends in the town of Bethany.

A Time to Rest

Mary knows her sister Martha isn't happy. Their small house is filled with company, and the honored guest is Jesus himself, the One they call Lord.

When Jesus sits down and begins to teach, Mary feels a pang of guilt. She should head back into the kitchen, where Martha is making a great clatter with platters, jars, and serving trays. Preparing even a small meal takes a lot of effort, and here is a houseful of people to feed.

But the words of Jesus flow like pure water to her thirsty soul, and Mary settles down at the Rabbi's feet, unable to tear herself away. Suddenly the noise and bustle of her busy day ebbs away, and Jesus' voice is all she can hear in the stillness. She sighs deeply and takes in the words and presence of her Master, some-how knowing this time is precious and rare.

Mary hears Martha's grumbling from the kitchen, but she tries to ignore it. Then Martha bursts through the crowd, and her anger cannot be ignored any longer. Her face is red and sweaty as she looks at Jesus and points to her sister. "Lord, don't you care that my sister has left me to do the work by myself? Tell her to help me!"

Mary and Martha ... needed to stop doing and start being—being children of God.

Mary feels herself flush with shame and embarrassment. She wants to stand and run out of the room, but her body feels frozen in place as she waits to hear words of reprimand. Instead, Jesus' voice is tender and calm.

"Martha, Martha," he says. "You are worried and upset about many things, but only one thing is needed. Mary has chosen what is better, and it will not be taken away from her."

Mary's tense muscles relax and she is overwhelmed with a deep peace, the kind she has only ever known in the presence of her Lord. She shuffles to the side, makes space for Martha, and pats the floor next to her. With one last look toward the kitchen, Martha wipes her damp brow, then sinks humbly to join her sister on the floor at Jesus' feet. Her eyes are wet and her glance at Mary is filled with an unspoken request: *Forgive me.*

Mary takes her sister's hand and together they rest in the cool refreshment that pours from the heart of their Master.

Where to Find the Fruit of Peace

For busy Mary and Martha, peace came at the feet of Jesus. They each needed to stop *doing* and start *being*—being children of God, at home in the love of his Son. Can we find the path to peace in our daily lives in the same way?

The biblical account in Luke 10:38–42 does not tell us how Martha responded to Jesus' correction, but I like to hope that she listened to him and changed her direction. If she had gone back about her business, she would have missed an opportunity that might never have come again. Imagine getting to rest at the very feet of Jesus and absorb his words meant just for you.

The good news is that we have that special opportunity each day, and we will have it forever in eternity. The bad news is

Jesus promises an inner peace to those who choose to follow him.

that we allow other demands in our lives to pull us away from Jesus and time in his presence.

The good news is that each day we can try to change and make room for the peace he wants to give us. Making that room can very closely resemble rest.

Rest is one of our most basic needs.

Remember that during his earthly life, Jesus indulged in physical rest, even in the midst of a heavy ministry schedule. Think about the time he napped in the boat, waking up just in time to still the waves of the stormy sea. (See Matt. 8:24.)

Jesus also promises an inner peace, rest, and renewal to those who choose to follow him. "Come to Me, all who are weary and heavy-laden, and I will give you rest.... For My yoke is easy and My burden is light" (Matt. 11:28, 30 NASB).

Martha of Bethany was a person who—like me—didn't know how to rest. When Jesus came to visit, Martha scurried around, trying to get a meal ready and pressuring her sister to do the same. Mary, with a different set of priorities, put off doing the work to rest at Jesus' feet and listen to him. Jesus commended her for that.

Rest is one of our most basic needs. Without it, it is very difficult both to have peace and to share that peace with others. But today's fast-paced lifestyle puts rest far down on the list of important tasks. Sometimes we even feel self-righteous about giving up rest in order to do more for our jobs, our family members, our church, and our volunteer activities. That feeling of sacrifice and self-satisfaction might keep us going for a while. Without rest, adrenaline kicks in to help us check off every item on the list, get to every meeting and appointment, and push forward to that indefinable day when we can say, "Whew! Now that's done and I can take a break."

Ultimately the adrenaline wears off, and we can be left with burnout, emptiness, even depression. The well has gone dry because we didn't stop for a refill of living Water.

What kind of importance do you place on rest in your world? If you drew a continuum—a line with Mary on one side and Martha on the other—would you be at the feet of Jesus like Mary, or in the kitchen with Martha? Where do you want to be?

And what if you are, right now, in the middle of intense stress, the kind brought on by job or financial losses, shattered relationships, illness, or loss of a loved one? Where do you find peace when your heart is fearful or aching?

I was recently inspired by the peace illustrated in the life of a man I don't even know. When he faced serious heart surgery, this e-mail was circulated to those of us who could pray for him:

Dear Brothers and Sisters,

I have daily devotions with each of my classes at our Christian High School. We say Shema, recite a verse or two, and I share a brief devotional. The week before spring break I chose

Habakkuk 3:19, probably words of David
(2 Samuel 22:34), "Make my feet like the feet of a
deer." I shared what God taught me in Israel
regarding this verse. The deer of the desert where
David was hiding are the Ibex of mountain goats.
They can climb nearly impossible vertical paths
without falling because they have the perfect feet.
They have been given a very tough path but can
handle it because of the feet God has given them.
I encouraged students to trust God's choice of path
and to seek His gift of the right feet for the path.

That devotion moment was for me too.
During the vacation, as part of my annual physical, my physicians found significant blockage in
the arteries of my heart. Monday I meet with a
surgeon to schedule a heart bypass as soon as
possible. The path God has given me has come to
some rough terrain. I am seeking His gift of the
appropriate feet. I do not know where the path
leads. I have much I would love to continue to do
in my ministry and with my family. I believe that
is His will too. If not, I do not question the path;
I only seek His gift of feet.

I share this part of my journey with you for a
couple of reasons. I desire you to pray with me for
those feet. God has already answered my prayers
for healing (I have the best medical team one
could ask for), and for peace (I am sure the path
is the one He wishes for me).

Please pray for my family. They carry the
burden of worry for me as husband, dad, and
grampa. Pray God will teach them (through me)
how to walk the tough parts of life's path, and
that they will see the presence of God in every
step. Pray my grandkids will remember my walk
with Jesus whatever turn the path takes.

Please pray for me. I have the peace of knowing I am in God's hands. The evil one (cursed be he) would rob me of that. Pray I will know God's promised presence every step. Pray that the surgeons would be His instruments and that He would be glorified (hopefully in healing of course) whatever the path. Pray for the patience I will need to regain strength and to reclaim my "boundary lines" (Psalm 16:6) soon.

I also share this with you to encourage you in knowing that I still seek to walk as Jesus walked and this has only strengthened my resolve to do so. Do not be discouraged or dismayed. His path leads to life and blessing. And He will provide feet for you and for me.

Taking time for deliberate rest can help us practice the presence of God.

My heart was lifted when I received this e-mail because it showed so clearly that peace comes from trusting God to give us what we need. Not knowing the outcome, this man of faith faced the future and gave it over to his Lord. The surgery turned out well and the man is now recovering, but he felt peaceful about his future, regardless.

Peace in Action

We tend not to put the words *peace* and *action* together, probably because peace often connotes stillness and quiet rather than activity; rest rather than motion. Yet it's important to consider those verbs—the action words—that may help us to experience peace in the middle of our fast-paced daily lives.

Taking time for quiet moments and deliberate rest can help us practice the presence of God and faithfully follow him—as did King David. While David was a fighter, a mover, and a shaker, he also had a tremendous grasp of the real peace that comes from time spent in conversation with his Lord.

The psalms of David reveal how honest the communication was between this man and his Maker. David understood that God is involved in each detail of our lives and deeply and personally concerned about all aspects of daily living. David fully committed his life into God's hands. You can see his attitude reflected in the following verses:

> O LORD, you have searched me
>   and you know me.
> You know when I sit and when I rise;
>   you perceive my thoughts from afar.
> You discern my going out and my lying down;
>   you are familiar with all my ways.
> Before a word is on my tongue
>   you know it completely, O LORD....
> Where can I go from your Spirit?

> Where can I flee from your presence?
> If I go up to the heavens, you are there;
>> if I make my bed in the depths, you
>> are there.
> If I rise on the wings of the dawn,
>> if I settle on the far side of the sea,
> even there your hand will guide me,
>> your right hand will hold me fast.
> (Ps. 139:1–4, 7–10)

David recognized that God knew his very thoughts and his words before he could even speak them. There is nowhere that is out of reach of God's presence and his upholding, guiding hand.

Further into Psalm 139, David praises God for creating him and molding him: "For you created my inmost being; you knit me together in my mother's womb. I praise you because I am fearfully and wonderfully made" (vv. 13–14).

While later in the psalm David asks for God to help him battle their mutual enemies, he ends with an affirmation of his total trust and devotion:

> Search me, O God, and know my heart;
>> test me and know my anxious thoughts.
> See if there is any offensive way in me,
>> and lead me in the way everlasting.
> (Ps. 139:23–24)

Though David was far from perfect and had sinned blatantly against the Lord, he was willing to put himself in God's hands and be led into the future, whatever it might hold. To me, that is an example of true peace in action.

Another illustration of peace painted in the Psalms is found in the elegant imagery of Psalm 23. Here David, the former shepherd boy, takes the role of the sheep protected and nurtured by a loving Shepherd. Who can read these words and not feel the assurance which lies beneath them?

> The LORD is my shepherd, I shall not be in
>   want.
> He makes me lie down in green pastures,
>   he leads me beside quiet waters,
>   he restores my soul.
> He guides me in paths of righteousness
>   for his name's sake.
> Even though I walk
>   through the valley of the shadow of death,
> I will fear no evil,
>   for you are with me;
> your rod and your staff,
>   they comfort me.
> You prepare a table before me
>   in the presence of my enemies.
> You anoint my head with oil;
>   my cup overflows.
> Surely goodness and love will follow me
>   all the days of my life,
> and I will dwell in the house of the LORD forever.

When I was a young girl of eight or nine, I memorized this psalm—but in its more poetic expression from the King James version. Over the decades it has come back to me—at the bedside of my dying grandmother, during my son's hard-won battle with bone cancer, alone in a hospital bed after my own mastectomy. Each time David's words bring me peace and restore my soul as I remember that the Shepherd is always in charge of my life and cares for me infinitely.

Gardener's Tools for Life

What are some practical means for bearing the fruit of peace in our lives? Here are several ideas to help you nurture peace in the midst of a demanding and busy life. These steps include

- choosing to manage your external world
- making room for rest
- cultivating mindfulness

How do you manage your external world to create an environment of peace and not chaos or stress? For some of you, it's easier than for others. The de-clutterers among us, for instance, at least know they can find what they're looking for—which means they have one less distraction in this sensory-overloaded life. I know I feel more internally peaceful when my counter is clear and the floor isn't being used by my kids as the largest shelf in the house.

While I'm tempted to say that living without kids is just naturally more peaceful, I know that's not really true. A single friend with a caring heart has filled her home with cats and more than a hundred houseplants. She stays busy cleaning, feeding, and loving her charges in her very full house. She's also busy trying to earn a living, so her choice to fill her world with animals and greenery must give her fulfillment that balances the extra workload.

The stress-inducing task of taking my boys to school each morning can be a time filled with arguments and anxiety. (Picture driving grouchy, sleep-deprived teens through a crowded high school parking lot filled with frustrated parents late for work and sixteen-year-old daredevil drivers.) At least the CD playing acoustic guitar music helps soothe us and calm the crazed rush threatening to ruin our day before it even begins. We could also drive in grim silence or crank up the hard rock radio station (the better to get that sluggish blood pumping). I suppose I could sing a few hymns; "It Is Well with My Soul" comes to mind. But the boys despise my singing, so we've settled on making our Buick a little haven of peace at the dawn of the day. For a few minutes anyway.

> *You need to rest—to peacefully refresh the inner you.*

Do you leave room for rest in your life? Don't feel guilty about resting instead of doing chores, catching up on e-mail, or running errands. Sometimes when I take time for myself, I cancel the benefits by worrying about what I *should* be doing. Remember, you need to rest—to peacefully refresh the inner you as well as your relationships with family, friends, and God.

Plan specific times for physical and spiritual renewal. Be realistic about your time. Maybe you can give yourself only ten minutes a day. But maybe you have an hour. Schedule a consistent "time out" that you can count on and look forward to each day.

Weed out distractions. Don't try to entertain yourself by turning on the TV or computer. You need to eliminate some of life's excess input, not add more.

You may find it helps you focus your thoughts by reading the Bible or a devotional book, listening to music, or writing in a journal. But be sure to allow yourself some silence so you can reflect, respond, and pray.

Discover what is especially relaxing for you. Some people enjoy a cup of hot tea, others want a lapful of knitting. Maybe a certain chair or special corner helps you escape from daily concerns. Develop a routine of relaxation.

Work on a state of mindfulness. What is that? Well, I'll tell you what it isn't. It is not allowing your mind to be so full of to-do lists and inner dialogue that you lose track of your actions.

Here's an example. I was headed down the stairs and toward a meeting room at church when I noticed the lobby was dotted with randomly positioned chairs. They were empty chairs, mini-chairs from the kids' classrooms, and there were no people in sight. *Is this some sort of new performance-art?* I wondered. *It can't be performance art, because there's nobody around actually performing. What is this display?*

My mind happily wandered down this trivial and fruitless path, stuck on pondering some kind of obscure modern art, when I took out my keys to unlock the meeting room door. I had to laugh out loud at myself when I came back to reality and realized I was pointing my car key remote at the room door and uselessly pushing the "unlock" button.

These days it takes only a moment's mental vacation before I wake up in crazyland. In this world of easy distraction, I need to pay better attention to my actions. I must learn to cultivate mindfulness, being more in the moment and less in my head. Not only will I find the right keys for unlocking doors, but I just might tap into the peace that so easily eludes me.

And when anxiety attacks, I can wrap myself in a cloak of serenity for protection. That cloak is woven of deliberate mindfulness regarding the presence of God in my life and his love and power to care for me. Those reminders are so helpful in combating the fears that rob me of peace.

If you're like me, you may need to relearn the art of making room for rest and peace in your life. Don't feel it's a luxury. It's a habit that can lend strength for the demands of daily life. Peace is a fruit of the Spirit, a gift from God that should be cultivated by each of us for his glory.

Allow the following Scripture passages and hymn lyrics to sink into your mind and heart, and help bring forth the fruit of peace during these busy days. Meditate on them over the course of the next week.

> Trust in the LORD and do good;
>> dwell in the land and enjoy safe pasture.
> Delight yourself in the LORD
>> and he will give you the desires of your
>> heart.
> Commit your way to the LORD;
>> trust in him and he will do this:
> He will make your righteousness shine like
>> the dawn,
>> the justice of your cause like the noon
>> day sun.
> Be still before the LORD and wait patiently
>> for him;
>> do not fret when men succeed in their
>> ways,
>> when they carry out their wicked
>> schemes.
> (Ps. 37:3–7)

> Come, all you who are thirsty, come to the
>> waters;
> and you who have no money,
>> come, buy and eat!
> Come, buy wine and milk without money and
>> without cost.
> Why spend money on what is not bread,
>> and your labor on what does not satisfy?

Listen, listen to me, and eat what is good,
    and your soul will delight in the richest
      of fare.
Give ear and come to me;
    hear me, that your soul may live....
You will go out in joy and be led forth in
    peace;
    the mountains and hills will burst into
      song before you,
    and all the trees of the field will clap
      their hands.
(Isa. 55:1–3, 12)

IT IS WELL WITH MY SOUL (VERSES 1, 2, 4)
BY HORATIO G. SPAFFORD, 1873

When peace, like a river, attendeth my way,
When sorrows like sea billows roll;
Whatever my lot, Thou hast taught me to say,
It is well, it is well, with my soul.

Though Satan should buffet, though trials
    should come,
Let this blest assurance control,
That Christ has regarded my helpless estate,
And hath shed His own blood for my soul.

And, Lord, haste the day when my faith shall
    be sight,
The clouds be rolled back as a scroll;
The trump shall resound, and the Lord shall
    descend,
Even so, it is well with my soul.

Chapter 4

The Fruit of the Spirit Is ...
Patience

I used to think of myself as the poster child of patience.

After all, when I taught high school English to the "tough kids," I kept my cool, even when fights broke out in my classroom. I stuck with the task of teaching them basic spelling and grammar, and a few kids even emerged from that class able to write a decent sentence, complete with subject and verb.

And back in my college days, didn't I remain patient and encouraging while teaching the Charleston to movement-challenged actors appearing in a 1920s musical? It must have taken at least a hundred repetitions of "step-bend-tap-bend-back-bend-tap-bend" to achieve even a pale imitation of that once-popular dance step. But I resisted the temptation to quit, and eventually they got it. More or less. Well, a few looked like manic robots, but at least they all moved together.

I was also famous for my patience as a teacher of Sunday school toddlers. My husband, John, and I invented the game of "Jericho," where the kids would pile cardboard bricks on a round table, then march around it while we sang "Joshua Fit de Battle of Jericho." When the song stopped, they got to knock down the wall. Of course, they wanted to play again. And again. And again. It was so popular, one little boy later told his mother, "We had fun. I really like Mrs. ... uh ... Mrs. ... um ... Mrs. Turtle!" (I guess that's pretty close to "Mrs. Duckworth" for a three-year-old.)

It's easy to be patient when life is easy.

As a teacher or choreographer or director, I seemed to have an unlimited well of patience. So, naturally I thought of myself as a wonderfully patient person.

And then I had twins.

How often did I lose it as a mother? Let me count the ways. I'm sure the neighbors enjoyed the sight of me returning with my eighteen-month-old boys after a short jaunt to the corner of our block. Chris and Jon wanted to try to take their Big Wheels into the street: a big No-No. When they wouldn't follow my orders to stay on the sidewalk, I threatened to end the trike trip. At that point they melted down, and so did I. I ended up carrying two screaming, kicking toddlers—each slung over a shoulder—all the way back to our house for a time out. Good thing I didn't have triplets, or I would have had to balance that third child on my head.

It's hard when the going gets tough.

Have you heard of the "Terrible Twos"? My boys stretched out that infamous childhood phase, starting at a year-and-a-half and not wrapping up until they were at least three. They must have worked out some sort of schedule because one or the other threw a major tantrum each day during that memorable time. Usually they alternated, though some days they both blew up.

I read all the books and tried all the techniques. I put them in a safe place and ignored the fits. Or I held them close, looking lovingly into their eyes while they yelled at the top of their healthy lungs. When Chris became furious, he would stiffen his little body like a board and throw himself over backward. I'd pick him up, holding him out in front like a tea tray and try to get him to relax. They wouldn't end those tantrums until they were good and ready. Neither one ever melted into sorrowful tears as one book promised they would. They just vented until they were spent.

How hard I tried to be Donna Reed. How often I failed. Once, after reading (and believing) several baby and child care books that said we should let little ones help us in the kitchen, I let the boys assist me while I baked banana muffins. I stood Chris on a chair to my left and Jon on a chair to my right. I let them crack eggs, pour in the oil, and empty the cups of flour into the bowl. It was going so beautifully; we were a Norman Rockwell painting in motion.

But at the last possible moment, just before we mixed the batter, Chris lost his balance on the chair. I reached for him while he tried to steady himself … by grabbing the edge of the mixing bowl. As it flipped into the air, powdery flour flew everywhere and rained down on the three of us. In my head I could hear the mocking laughter of the Pillsbury Doughboy, scoffing at me for trying to bake from scratch.

I truly knew how far I'd fallen during one typical dinnertime scene with toddler twins. While they fussed and fumed in their high chairs, hungry and cranky, I alternated between working up their supper and trying to keep them pacified. Finally, I plopped down on a kitchen chair, slapped my hand on the table, and shouted, "How can you expect me to fix your dinner when you can't leave me alone!"

I don't know what I expected them to say. They were only two. At that moment I realized how little patience I had. I just crumbled and cried. Everybody has a breaking point, and I'd reached mine. Never again would I see myself as a well of endless patience. It had only been an illusion anyway. It's easy to be patient when life is easy. It's hard when the going gets tough.

I've made a few inquiries, and guess what? I'm not the only parent to lose it once in a while. Of course, nonparents also find their patience stretched past their personal limits. Still, I don't know what it is about parenthood, but inevitably it tests even the best-intentioned. A friend of mine shared this story about her friend, someone humble enough to expose her lack of patience under fire:

Charmaine, a mom living in South Africa at the time, picked up her seven-year-old daughter at school. Already in the car was a four-year-old—and a Barbie doll, a very exclusive item in South Africa. As the battle for the Barbie escalated, Charmaine gave the girls the ultimate warning: Stop the fighting or the doll goes out the window. But the girls failed to take heed.

She started driving faster to get home before she killed them both, all the while yelling, "I am warning you two." Forty miles an hour, fifty miles an hour: "I am going to throw that thing out the window if you don't stop it!"

At seventy miles an hour, her arm whipped back like Elastic Woman. She ripped the doll out of their grubby little paws and hurled it out the window. She looked in the rear view mirror. Their eyes were huge and their hands still in the air where the Barbie had been a nanosecond ago. End of conflict.

I guess a lot of moms struggle with patience. What happens when that fabled patience gives out? Here are a few incidents from a *Rocky Mountain News* article that show what can happen:

- A mother ignored her three-year-old because she thought he was fantasizing when he said "a birdie" lived in his room. One evening she walked in to discover a bat circling over the bed.

> *Patience is a fruit that can be refreshing and sweet, offering unexpected rewards.*

- A mother became impatient and insisted her child stop yelling for her from across the house and come into the kitchen to tell her what was wrong. The child showed up a few moments later, dripping wet. "I fell in the toilet," she wailed.
- An exhausted mother let her sleepless child "cry it out" through the night. At about 2 a.m. the wailing stopped. When the mom came into the room at daybreak, the one-year-old was asleep on the crib rail, one leg dangling on each side.
- An impatient mother dismissed her preschooler's limp as hypochondria for three days before taking her to the pediatrician, who told her the child had suffered a minor fracture.

When patience wears thin, it's not a pretty sight.

Time has passed and my boys have now grown into teenagers. They seem to have inherited much from me, including my lack of patience and lack of insight about it. Not long ago, Chris had to write a paper about his three best character traits. At the top of the list were the words, "I am patient."

"Where did you come up with this?" I asked him. "You're one of the least patient people I know."

"Yeah, I guess I am," he admitted. "But I thought it was something I should write about." Already he had picked up the idea that patience was something to be applauded. But actually practicing it in real life? That's another story altogether.

What's the toughest fruit in the grocery store? Not those wimpy bananas and peaches, so easily dented and bruised. Maybe it's watermelon, protected by its thick, green rind.

What's the toughest fruit of the Spirit? For many of us, it's patience.

Yet patience is a fruit that can be refreshing and sweet,

In our fast-paced culture, patience is becoming a rare treasure.

offering unexpected rewards. An example comes from my friend Doris, who had to deliberately practice patience in a difficult place, little knowing what it might bring forth.

One of my first careers was in the human services field. I worked in a juvenile detention center for a number of years, and in that time my patience was tried on many occasions. In one case my patience paid off.

A young man had gotten into a fight and had been escorted to his room to cool off. I went down to talk with him and find out what had caused the problem. After opening the door to his room, I asked my question.

He moved to the opposite side of the room next to the barred window. His words were, "You better leave for I don't want to hurt you."

I told him I had no intention of leaving and proceeded to stand in the doorway for nearly twenty minutes. During that time he just stood there, saying nothing. I didn't speak either. He also didn't move any closer or make any threatening moves.

Eventually he started to talk, and I began to understand what had caused the fight.

As a result of my patience during those tense minutes, when the young man returned to the facility time after time and eventually stayed for a number of months, I became his lifeline. He would be able to maintain and not fight as long as I was there to talk and listen to him. If I was not there, I would return to find out he was in lock up for fighting. He told me one time that he could not handle it when I was not there.

I always wondered if the others had taken the time to be patient and listen and not limit the time of listening if we could have kept him out of fights altogether.

In our instant-gratification, quick-answer, fast-paced culture, patience is becoming a rare treasure. We don't see a lot of examples rivaling Doris's story these days. So let's look back in time to study one sure model of patience during chaotic and trying times.

A Model of Patience

Leah clutches Samuel's hand tightly, knowing her little brother could easily be lost in the crowd if he should slip away. Just moments ago, Mother was standing beside them, trying to peek over the heads of taller adults pressing in around the Rabbi Jesus. But a heavy-set man pushed between them, and now Mother is nowhere to be seen.

Many grownups surrounding them have children in their arms or perched on their shoulders. Leah's mother had said she wanted to have her two children be blessed today by Jesus. But now the air is thick with dust, the space jammed with sweaty bodies, and Leah just wants to find her mother and leave. It is, however, impossible to turn around.

Loud voices rise above the crowd's murmur. "Away. Back away, you people. Lord, tell them to leave and take these crying babies with them."

Just then, the adults in front of Leah and Samuel begin to step aside, and she has a clear view of a man with strong shoulders and kind eyes. As he gently places an infant into its mother's arms, he shines his warm smile directly at Leah.

Then he quickly glances at the men who had been shouting orders. He tells them, "Let the little children come to me, and do not hinder them, for the kingdom of God belongs to such as these. I tell you the truth, anyone who will not receive the kingdom of God like a little child will never enter it" (Mark 10:14–15).

At that he looks down again at Leah, then crouches to pick up little Samuel. He stands with the boy wrapped in one arm while he places his other hand on Leah's head. His touch is tender. Time slows as he blesses the two children. He finishes speaking as Mother breaks through the now still crowd.

As she reaches for Samuel, "Thank you," is all she can manage to say. Jesus smiles again before turning and offering his loving touch to anyone else who needs it.

The happiness that has melted into Leah's heart feels as if it will stay there for a long, long time.

During his ministry here on earth, Jesus often showed patience, both to the crowds who were sometimes desperately drawn to him, and also to his disciples, who often got it wrong.

While the disciples no doubt meant well, their efforts at crowd control actually diverted Jesus from his important task: to demonstrate the kingdom of God and share his love. And this story from Mark 10 wasn't even the first example of the disciples heading off in the wrong direction and trying their Leader's patience.

Just a few verses prior to Mark's account of Jesus and the children, we read that the disciples had been arguing like little kids over who gets to go first: "They came to Capernaum. When he [Jesus] was in the house, he asked them, 'What were you arguing about on the road?'

It's encouraging to know that Jesus is patient with us as we take our faltering steps.

But they kept quiet because on the way they had argued about who was the greatest. Sitting down, Jesus called the Twelve and said, 'If anyone wants to be first, he must be the very last, and the servant of all'" (Mark 9:33–35).

Soon after that, the disciple John reveals another rash—and wrong—move. "'Teacher,' said John, 'we saw a man driving out demons in your name and we told him to stop, because he was not one of us.'

"'Do not stop him,' Jesus said. 'No one who does a miracle in my name can in the next moment say anything bad about me, for whoever is not against us is for us. I tell you the truth, anyone who gives you a cup of water in my name because you belong to Christ will certainly not lose his reward'" (Mark 9:38–41).

Ever the patient teacher, Jesus set his disciples straight time and again. Yes, the Gospels frequently show how that patience was tested and frayed, but the Lord did not give up on his followers, no matter how self-centered and slow they could be. It's encouraging to know that he is just as patient with us as we take our faltering and sometimes baby steps in our own life journeys.

The Fruit of Patience in an Impatient World

Patience grows as we learn to content ourselves with last place.

In addition to the cultural conditioning that short circuits our patience, what causes us to be impatient? One key lies in the Scripture passage above—Mark 9:35. We are impatient because we want to be first: first in line, first for the job, first to be waited on. Patience will only grow as we learn to content ourselves with last place.

That is terribly countercultural. We might end up last, but we don't usually feel happy about it. It takes a major shift in our thinking and attitudes to find acceptance in being the "servant of all." It requires us to keep in mind just who we are in relation to the Father who made us and who sustains us. And that can be difficult when you already feel too busy, overworked, underpaid and, basically, like a put-upon Cinderella starring in a not-so-fairy-tale life. When do you get to climb out of the ashes and put on the pretty dress?

It takes a supernatural attitude adjustment to bear the fruit of patience.

Waiting is never easy. Waiting on others seems even worse.

That's where the Holy Spirit comes in. It takes a supernatural attitude adjustment to bear the fruit of patience in a world that rewards the opposite. We need to lean on the Spirit and ask for help and humble hearts. As we yield to his guidance in our lives, we will find space for patience in this crowded life.

Patience in Action

Patience is a word that seems more about stillness and waiting than taking action. But a state of patience can require great acts of trust, self-control, and humility. An ideal example from Scripture comes from the life of a simple woman named Hannah.

I personally identify with Hannah because she endured the long drought of infertility, something I struggled with for seven years. Many women encounter some form of infertility these days, ranging from slight difficulty conceiving to having to endure extreme medical procedures to the pain of miscarriage.

The heartbreak of infertility was made even worse for Hannah because in ancient times women were mostly valued for their childbearing capability, and barrenness was thought to be punishment for sin.

Hannah's story is told in the book of 1 Samuel, beginning in chapter 1.

Though Hannah was loved greatly by her husband, Elkanah, she was not so greatly loved by his other wife, Peninnah. Because the Lord had closed Hannah's womb, Peninnah felt superior, blessed as she was with children. Hannah had to endure her rival's taunts and criticisms through year after year of barrenness.

Whenever Hannah went with her family to the house of the Lord, Peninnah provoked her until she wept and could not even eat.

Elkanah tried to help. "Why are you weeping? Why don't you eat? Why are you downhearted? Don't I mean more to you than ten sons?" His kindness only made her feel worse about her inability to give him children.

One particular visit to the temple finally pushed Hannah over the edge. She decided she would pray there until she had an answer. From the depths of her soul she wept and cried out to the Lord, saying, "O LORD Almighty, if you will only look upon your servant's misery and remember me, and not forget your servant but give her a son, then I will give him to the LORD for all the days of his life, and no razor will every be used on his head."

Hannah determined that if God answered her prayer, her son would become a Nazarite, wearing his hair long as a sign of being set aside to perform a special service to God.

From the temple doorway, the priest Eli watched the woman. All he could observe was a woman in great distress, moving her lips, her voice inaudible. To him, she appeared drunk. He had to confront her about this disgrace. "How long will you keep on getting drunk? Get rid of your wine."

Hannah replied, "I have not been drinking wine or beer; I was pouring out my soul to the LORD. Do not take your servant for a wicked woman; I have been praying here out of my great anguish and grief."

Eli answered, "Go in peace, and may the God of Israel grant you what you have asked of him."

She said, "May your servant find favor in your eyes."

Hannah's heart lifted as she departed, and for the first time in days she felt hungry enough to eat something.

In due time Hannah conceived a son. She named him Samuel, saying, "Because I asked the LORD for him." And true to her promise, when Samuel was three years old, she dedicated him to the tabernacle for life-long service to God.

Hannah waited on God, but she was not passive in the process. Because of her patience, she did not give up but sought continually to fulfill what God had planned for her. She was honest about her feelings and the grief she underwent as she longed for motherhood. She didn't try to suppress or deny her desires but brought them honestly to the Lord.

When Hannah presented her son to Eli for a life of service to God, she prayed a prayer of rejoicing. Her words reflect her deep awareness of God's sovereignty in her life and the role he played in her deliverance:

> My heart rejoices in the LORD;
> > in the LORD my horn is lifted high.
> My mouth boasts over my enemies,
> > for I delight in your deliverance.
> There is no one holy like the LORD;
> > there is no one besides you;
> > there is no Rock like our God....
> The bows of the warriors are broken,
> > but those who stumbled are armed with
> > > strength.
> Those who were full hire themselves out for
> > food,
> > but those who were hungry hunger no
> > > more.
> She who was barren has borne seven children,
> > but she who has had many sons pines
> > > away....
> For the foundations of the earth are the LORD's;
> > upon them he has set the world.
> He will guard the feet of his saints,
> > but the wicked will be silenced in
> > > darkness.

It is not by strength that one prevails;
 those who oppose the LORD will be
 shattered.
He will thunder against them from heaven;
 the LORD will judge the ends of the earth.
He will give strength to his king
 and exalt the horn of his anointed.
 (1 Sam. 2:1–2, 4–5, 8–10)

Hannah recognized that "it is not by strength that one prevails," but that God's will determines the outcome of life's struggles. Because she chose to depend humbly on him, her patience and trust were richly rewarded.

Gardener's Tools for Life

What kinds of things are you waiting for? If you had to make a list of ten things you must wait for, what would you list? Write as many as you can in your journal.

Once, during family night, we asked our kids to write such a list, and here's what one of them came up with:

1. Movie
2. Dinner
3. Grades
4. Other food
5. TV shows
6. Games
7. Jesus to come back to earth
8. Friends to come over
9. Amusement park rides
10. Sleep after a hard day

Your own list might be just that simple, or much more complicated. In the past my list has contained such varied items as waiting for:

1. My wedding day after a year-long engagement
2. An end to a bad job
3. The beginning of a good job
4. Buying a house
5. An end to infertility
6. A happy ending to a high-risk pregnancy
7. My child (Chris) to be cured of cancer
8. My own remission from breast cancer
9. Answers to unanswerable questions
10. An end to endless waiting

Why don't you take a few minutes to write in your journal a list of ten things for which you have waited or are waiting now? Then rate yourself on a patience scale of one to ten as you evaluate the level of your patience. Pause and pray for those items that evoke impatience. Ask God to help you trust him for the outcome.

Think about those times you most easily lose patience. Do you have problems when you're stuck in traffic or being cut off by rude and rushed drivers? Do you ever yell at other drivers when you're behind the wheel? How about in private, when you're the only one in the car? I admit, I've had my limitations in this area!

One thing that helps me today when I'm frustrated with other drivers is to try to put myself in their shoes. Maybe they are distracted because of a recent loss or family disaster. Maybe the problem is inexperience. Now that I have two drivers to teach, just a few weeks away from getting their permits, I am much more understanding when I see a young person driving hesitantly or making too-sudden moves.

In that same way, try to look at whatever burns your patience fuse in a different way. Can you give others the benefit of the doubt? Even if they are being pushy or taking your place from you, ask yourself: *What really is my rightful place?* According to Jesus, it's at the end of the line. Next time you're in the grocery store line, behind somebody paying all in coins or unloading thirty-five items in the twelve-or-under line, remember that the fruit of the Spirit is patience. Say a silent prayer for the people ahead of you, especially the obnoxious ones because they probably need it the most.

Take time this week to read and meditate on the following verses. Ask God to burn them on your heart, so they will rise to mind during the tough times when patience seems in short supply.

> Be patient, then, brothers, until the Lord's coming. See how the farmer waits for the land to yield its valuable crop and how patient he is for

the autumn and spring rains. You too, be patient
and stand firm, because the Lord's coming is
near. Don't grumble against each other, brothers,
or you will be judged. The Judge is standing at
the door!

Brothers, as an example of patience in the
face of suffering, take the prophets who spoke in
the name of the Lord. As you know, we consider
blessed those who have persevered. You have
heard of Job's perseverance and have seen what
the Lord finally brought about. The Lord is full
of compassion and mercy. (James 5:7–11)

> I am still confident of this:
> > I will see the goodness of the LORD
> > in the land of the living.
> Wait for the LORD;
> > be strong and take heart
> > and wait for the LORD. (Ps. 27:13–14)

And we pray this in order that you may live a life
worthy of the Lord and may please him in every
way: bearing fruit in every good work, growing in
the knowledge of God, being strengthened with
all power according to his glorious might so that
you may have great endurance and patience, and
joyfully giving thanks to the Father, who has
qualified you to share in the inheritance of the
saints in the kingdom of light. (Col. 1:10–12)

Chapter 5

The Fruit of the Spirit Is ...

Kindness

It was a very bleak winter for my son Chris and our entire family. Illinois winters can be harsh, but this one brought unique hardships. Though only five years old, Chris was fighting for his life as he underwent weekly chemotherapy treatments for bone cancer.

Regular hospital visits an hour and a half away from home and frequent five-day stays dominated our lives. Twin brother Jon never knew which parent would be home to take care of him, but it was seldom both at once. When Chris was home, we couldn't go anywhere as a family because low white-cell counts made him vulnerable to germs of any kind. It was all we could do to manage Chris's medical crisis, get Jon to kindergarten, and still stay employed. We made it to church only sporadically. Days were a blur of exhaustion and uncertainty.

> *Kindness has the power to bring light to darkness.*

Christmas was coming, and I didn't know how I'd find time to do any shopping. Planning for the holidays came far down on the list. Yet, as it turned out, an act of kindness meant I didn't have to worry about Christmas after all.

My friend Camille worked at the local school district office, which they called "the D.O." for short. She knew what our family was going through and told her colleagues about it. This caring group of people then took up a collection and planned a surprise: a visit from Santa Claus.

Camille called to ask if we minded surprising the boys with toys hand delivered by Santa, to be played by a staff member's husband who just loved any opportunity to be the jolly old elf. We were thrilled and set the date. "Don't buy the kids any toys yourself," suggested Camille. "They'll have plenty."

As Christmas neared, Chris and Jon worried that the space under the tree looked too bare. Then on the

Saturday before the holiday, the doorbell rang and in walked Santa Claus, bending under the weight of a huge bag. While the kids stared in semi-shock, he unloaded dozens of brightly wrapped packages. After building a small mountain of gifts around the base of our tree, he left us with a happy "Ho, ho, ho!"

Needless to say, that Christmas morning set a standard of abundance we've never been able to beat in all the years since. It took hours for the boys to open all those presents—two of everything. There were cars and games and cassette players with earphones. The presents were carefully selected and perfect for two active five-year-olds. For John and me, this card, with a poem written by Carol Boyle, told the tale behind the scenes:

> 'Twas the week before Christmas and
>   throughout the D.O.
> We went through the motions, we tied
>   every bow.
> Up went the fireplace, up went the tree,
> But lo and behold—we were missing the
>   glee.
> Then out came a story of a family quite
>   near,
> With two little boys so precious and dear.
> When we thought of the year this family
>   lived through,
> We knew our gifts many and troubles were
>   few.
> We elves went to work with a lighthearted
>   spark.

On a mission of love did the office
   embark.
And what before our wondering eyes
   should appear ...
But smiles and laughter and happiness
   clear.
Within the blink of an eye, Santa's bag
   was quite laden,
To offer this Christmas as a few moments'
   haven.
Please accept these gifts with all the love
   they are filled.
And we thank your dear family for the
   spirit instilled.

That note brought me many tears of joy as I envisioned this caring group of people—all except Camille were complete strangers to us. I was so moved by the way they gave of themselves with total compassion for our family. Their act of kindness brought hope and joy that Christmas. At the same time, it seems to have lifted their hearts as well. What a beautiful expression of the true meaning of Christmas.

Kindness has the power to bring light to darkness and warmth to a cold world. We hear so many news stories about the pain wrought by evil people, we need stories of kindness to provide an antidote to despair over the state of our world and the people in it.

How do you feel when you open your local paper and see a letter to the editor like this one from the Colorado Springs *Gazette*?

We would like to thank the gentleman who anonymously paid for our 60th anniversary dinner at the Olive Garden on July 28. We have no idea of his identity, as he was at a table behind us and overheard our conversation with the waitress about our anniversary. When he left, he paid for our meal including dessert. The waitress then told us what he had done.

All one reads or hears on the news is about the bad that happens in the world, and we wanted to pass on some good news that happened to us. There are good and kind people in our world, also. We wanted all to know that there are fine people out there and it was our pleasure to have been the recipients of his kindness.

Thank you, sir, whoever you are. And may God bless you.

Those letters always touch my heart and often bring tears to my eyes. Stories like this are a solid encouragement and a reminder that basic acts of kindness can make a huge difference to both individuals and communities. They demonstrate that empathy and compassion are not dead, but living in the hearts of people willing to care. These stories are part of a circle of kindness, motivating me to care also, to reach beyond my little life and try to make a difference in the lives of others.

Of the many word pictures painted of Jesus in the Bible, examples of his kindness and understanding stand out the most to me.

A Gift of Kindness, Given Humbly

She almost turns away at the doorway, knowing she is not likely to find welcome at the home of a Pharisee. But she has heard that Jesus will be here, and when a rabbi is invited to someone's house, it is customary for anyone to stop by and listen to the conversation. Even a woman of her reputation. *Perhaps they won't recognize me,* she thinks.

The alabaster jar of perfume is small, but feels unusually heavy in her hand as she moves toward the center of the room. She recognizes Jesus from the other day, when she heard him teach in the marketplace. Now he is reclining at the table, so she quietly stands behind him to better hear the words of hope that moved her so deeply before.

Soon she is weeping uncontrollably, drawn to the kingdom of God described by this wise Rabbi, and aware that she has lived far away from truth. Suddenly she is embarrassed to realize that her tears have dripped from her cheeks onto the dusty feet of Jesus. Crouching down, she uses her long hair to wipe them dry. To show her respect and affection, she kisses his feet, then pours the costly perfume over them. She refuses to think about the expense; she only desires to show how much he and his precious words of hope mean to her.

Jesus speaks to the Pharisee seated next to him, obviously the host of the banquet. "Simon, I have something to tell you."

"Tell me, teacher," replies Simon.

"Two men owed money to a certain moneylender. One owed him five hundred denarii, and the other fifty. Neither of them had the money to pay him back, so he canceled the debts of both. Now which of them will love him more?"

Simon answers, "I suppose the one who had the bigger debt canceled."

"You have judged correctly," Jesus says.

She feels the Rabbi's steady gaze before she actually realizes that his eyes are now fully upon her.

"Do you see this woman? I came into your house. You did not give me any water for my feet, but she wet my feet with her tears and wiped them with her hair. You did not give me a

True kindness is prompted by humility and not arrogance and power.

kiss, but this woman ... has not stopped kissing my feet. You did not put oil on my head, but she has poured perfume on my feet. Therefore, I tell you, her many sins have been forgiven—for she loved much. But he who has been forgiven little loves little."

She dares to stare directly into Jesus' eyes as he tells her, in the kindest voice she's ever known, "Your sins are forgiven.... Your faith has saved you; go in peace."

The warmth of forgiveness and Jesus' compassion fills her entire being. She rushes from the room, outdoors, where she finds a shady tree. Collapsing under its broad branches, she weeps aloud, releasing sweet tears of joy and relief. As she wipes her face with her hands, she catches the lingering scent of her spilled perfume, the fragrance of a new beginning and promised hope.

Showing kindness is not an act of law but a gesture of grace.

The circle of kindness is clearly drawn in this account taken from from Luke 7:36–50. We can see how the sinful woman approached Jesus on the basis of his teaching, trusting that he would not judge her scornfully but would extend kindness and compassion. Aware of the depth of her sin and the extent of the Lord's forgiveness, she responded with generosity and tenderness, caring for Jesus' feet in a cultural act of reverence and submission.

True kindness is prompted by humility and not arrogance and power. The Pharisee had the money and the position in his world. But he didn't yield them to Jesus. He didn't even provide the basic courtesy of a bowl of water so that Jesus might clean his dusty feet before dinner. Only the poor woman, probably a prostitute in the community, was willing to humble herself and wash Jesus' feet with her tears. Only she made a financial sacrifice by pouring out perfume, which must have cost a great deal for someone who had little in the way of financial resources. But she gave willingly and from her grateful heart.

Showing kindness is not an act of law but a gesture of grace. It should be as natural as breathing to those who understand the depth of the forgiveness offered by a loving heavenly Father. In return, acts of kindness reward us with the sort of joy we may only fully know in heaven—a taste of heaven on earth.

The apostle Paul encourages believers to show love and kindness to each other. In the book of Galatians, the same book that contains our key passage about the fruit of the Spirit, we read,

Yet basic kindness is always an option, even in tough times.

You, my brothers, were called to be free. But do not use your freedom to indulge the sinful nature; rather, serve one another in love. The entire law is summed up in a single command: "Love your neighbor as yourself." If you keep on biting and

devouring each other, watch out or you will be
destroyed by each other....

Carry each other's burdens, and in this way
you will fulfill the law of Christ.... Let us not
become weary in doing good, for at the proper
time we will reap a harvest if we do not give up.
Therefore, as we have opportunity, let us do
good to all people, especially to those who
belong to the family of believers. (Gal. 5:13–15;
6:2, 9–10)

I'm sorry to observe that it seems as though, even
in churches, compassion ministries have suffered
because of the accelerated pace of modern life and the
scramble to make a living. It's harder to find volunteers when the workweek continues to expand. Money
that might have gone to help others now is barely stretched to cover growing gas prices and steep house payments.

Give what you can—because you have been given much.

Yet basic kindness is always an option, even in tough times. It can be expressed as simply as allowing another driver to pull ahead of you. When kids sell candy or popcorn to raise money for a good cause, you may not have the budget to pay the full price for the fund-raiser, but maybe you have a dollar to spare and share. It could be that today, the only extra you have to offer is a kind word or a smile of encouragement as you encounter somebody even more stressed than you are.

The circle of kindness is drawn without thought for quantity or expense. Give what you can—because you have been given much—and you may find yourself equipped to give something you didn't even know you had.

In the case of my friend Afton, kindness came in the form of e-mails from someone she had only recently met. This is her story:

Empathy, encouragement, concern: They're all free.

My daughter thinks that while she works hard in school every day, I sit at my computer and play "Solitaire." To her, my job as a freelance writer and editor sounds so FUN. And some days, some years, it is. Other times it is sheer frustration.

Last September seemed particularly frustrating. My editing work had slowed down, and I had received multiple rejections for my children's book. I'd actually decided it was time to get a real job; I had even filled out a job application. Then when the snow started to fly, an editor-friend I hadn't heard from in several years e-mailed to ask if I would work with a first-time writer to sharpen the focus of her book. Yes!

I jumped into the project. I began an e-mail conversation with the author, Jan Coates. We wrote back and forth about words and God, but we also began to develop a friendship. Jan made it a point to ask about my teenagers. She sympathized with me when I had an emergency root canal. And then I happened to mention that I was writing a children's book and feeling very discouraged. She became my personal cheerleader. "Don't give up! Pull it out of the drawer. Let me give you the name of an agent I know. You go, Girl!"

Jan's book, *Set Free: God's Healing Power for Abuse Survivors and Those Who Love Them*, has now been published, but Jan and I still e-mail frequently. Recently she told me she dreamed I called her with news of a contract for my book.

Jan's kindness has forever marked my heart and given me new courage in my own writing. I wonder if God laughs, as I do, at the irony of it all. I was supposed to be the one helping this new author.

Afton's story is a wonderful illustration of the circle of kindness, of how the helper becomes the helped. And Jan's outreach didn't cost anything. Empathy, encouragement, concern: They're all free. They spill from a full heart into surrounding lives and require nothing more than an attitude of love and a willingness to give the Spirit room to move.

Kindness in Action

Acts of kindness seem more commonplace in times of abundance than in periods of want and deprivation. When time and resources are in short supply, kindness demands more of a sacrifice but can also return more of a blessing.

The story of the widow and the prophet Elijah from 1 Kings 17 demonstrates the power of a kind and sacrificial act.

The land was choked with drought and Elijah was running out of options when he arrived in the town of Zarephath. When he came to the town gate, he saw a widow there gathering sticks. He called to her and asked, "Would you bring me a little water in a jar so I may have a drink?"

The widow turned to assist the stranger in what little way she could, when he called out again. "And bring me, please, a piece of bread."

The widow sighed. Desperation etched her face. "As surely as the LORD your God lives, I don't have any bread—only a handful of flour in a jar and a little oil in a jug. I am gathering a few sticks to take home and make a meal for myself and my son, that we may eat it—and die."

Elijah said to her, "Don't be afraid. Go home and do as you have said. But first make a small cake of bread for me from what you have and bring it to me, and then make something for yourself and your son. For this is what the LORD, the God of Israel, says: 'The jar of flour will not be used up and the jug of oil will not run dry until the day the LORD gives rain on the land.'"

Kindness in action often involves risk-taking.

The woman hesitated for only a moment. Should she trust this strange-looking foreigner? She went away and did as he told her. Amazingly, there was food every day for Elijah and for the woman and her family. The jar of flour remained full and the jug of oil did not run dry, just as promised.

While the widow believed the plentiful food was reward enough for her kindness, she soon received an even greater gift of thanks.

When her beloved son fell ill and stopped breathing, she gathered the boy in her arms and carried him to Elijah. The prophet took the boy to an upper room and laid him on the bed. Then he cried out to the Lord, "O LORD my God, let this boy's life return to him!"

The Lord heard Elijah's cry and life returned to the boy. Picking him up, Elijah carried him down and gave him to his mother, saying, "Look, your son is alive!"

The woman replied in gratitude, "Now I know that you are a man of God and that the word of the LORD from your mouth is the truth."

The widow's kindness brought forth a great deal of fruit: food for the moment, renewed life for her son, and trust in the Lord for eternity. She took a risk in reaching out to a strange man during a time of want and deprivation. But her willingness to meet the needs of another person ended up changing her life forever.

Kindness in action often involves risk-taking, and the rewards are not always so obvious. Yet there is never a wrong time to extend grace to another human being, and the outcome is bound to be used of God to make this world a better place.

Gardener's Tools for Life

Ted Dreier is a friend of my parents and the head of Moozie's Kindness Foundation, a nonprofit foundation dedicated to "spreading the milk of human kindness." He presents special programs for children featuring Moozie the cow. I once observed one of his innovative presentations, captivating children with a full-sized fabric cow that comes out of a suitcase!

Since my mom is a cowboy poet, Ted asked her to tell the story of Moozie in a rhyming picture book. As a result of the Children's Kindness programs and the book *Moozie's Kind Adventure*, Ted's Web site (www.moozie.com) is full of comments from kids learning to practice kindness in very practical, but kidlike ways. Some of their suggestions and stories might tickle you as they did me:

- I wanted to write a poem for Moozie.
  Kindness: A true saying or a kind word.
  To listen to someone that needs to be
      heard.
  It is to tend to someone in need.
  Kindness can be helping or doing a good
      deed.
  You can make someone happy.
  Being friends with someone even if they
      are wacky.
  Make someone feel better by sharing.
  Overall be caring.
  Do what you think. Use your mind.
  Just go out there and be kind.
  If everyone was kind, one random act.
  Then this world wouldn't be packed
  With anger and tears.
  Or with sadness and fears.
  This world would be a better place just
      with kindness. (Kelsey, 12)

- I am five years old and live in Bayside.
  Yesterday I helped my grandma rake
  leaves. I love you Moozie and I will always
  continue to help people. (Lauren, 5)
- If you are kind people are kind to you
  back. And if you are kind you start to feel
  good inside. One day I was kind to a friend
  and now he can trust me. (Shawki, 7)
- I went to the food bank yesterday and
  helped out all of the people that were in
  there. It made me feel nice and warm and
  fuzzy inside. (Cindy, 9)
- I got carrots to share with the whole second
  grade for snack time! I love you, Moozie!

> You are a moognificant cow! (Lara, a
> teacher)

Take out your journal and think about the essence
of kindness. What defines kindness in your life? Write
a short poem about it. It doesn't have to be a great lit-
erary work. In fact, write the poem as if you were twelve
years old. Your challenge is to use simple words and
concepts to express an essential truth about kindness.

Spend time this week considering these verses
from the Bible:

> He who despises his neighbor sins,
>   but blessed is he who is kind to the
>   needy....
> He who oppresses the poor shows
>   contempt for their Maker,
>   but whoever is kind to the needy
>   honors God.
> (Prov. 14:21, 31)

> Do not let any unwholesome talk come out of
> your mouths, but only what is helpful for build-
> ing others up according to their needs, that it
> may benefit those who listen. And do not grieve
> the Holy Spirit of God, with whom you were
> sealed for the day of redemption. Get rid of all
> bitterness, rage and anger, brawling and slan-
> der, along with every form of malice. Be kind
> and compassionate to one another, forgiving
> each other, just as in Christ God forgave you.
> (Eph. 4:29–32)

Ask yourself this question: Do I need to forgive anyone today? If the answer is yes, begin the process of forgiveness.

> Be imitators of God, therefore, as dearly loved children and live a life of love, just as Christ loved us and gave himself up for us as a fragrant offering and sacrifice to God. (Eph. 5:1–2)

Chapter 6

The Fruit of the Spirit Is ...
Goodness

Novels, films, and stories in every form have repeatedly drawn upon the timeless theme of "good versus evil." From Shakespeare to Spielberg, from Beowulf to the Big Bad Wolf, from Peter Pan to Star Wars, our literature and entertainment echoes a universal truth: There is good and there is evil, and they do battle on every stage, in fiction and in reality, each and every day.

The original account of this ongoing, ever-present struggle is rooted in the book of Genesis, and grounded in the garden of Eden. God created the heavens and the earth, oceans and mountains, toads and toadstools, porpoises and people. He called all his creation "good"—until the serpent tried to undermine him, seducing mankind with the promise of power. Evil then closed the gates of the garden until Jesus made a way to open the door once again.

In present days when trouble comes and upends normal, ordered life, the lines between good and evil stand out in sharpest relief. A flood swamps a city and some survivors push their way to safety, threatening the weak, stealing from the defenseless. In the same city, others risk their lives to save endangered neighbors, share from meager food stocks, stay to help when it would be easier to leave. Inevitably, good people outnumber evil people, and the sacrifices of good people stand as an inspiration to everyone.

> *Goodness isn't just a state of being; it's a state of doing.*

When the world functions in an ordinary way, it's hard to see below the surface and into people's hearts. Most people can maintain a good appearance on the outside. But when life's regular pattern is disturbed, heroes arise and demonstrate a spirit of goodness in action. In my hometown, a devastating house fire exposed some truly good neighbors. Their story was reported in our local paper, the *Gazette*, on June 13, 2005.

A young woman, Calley Wenzel, was driving by her neighbor's house when she saw smoke. She jumped out of her car, ran in the garage and found sixty-two-year-old

Jimmie Kincheloe rushing out. Calley took the woman to her car and waited for emergency crews to arrive. Perhaps the story would have ended there, but for Calley's next-door neighbor, seventy-one-year-old Tossie Wilburn. She knew the fire victim had to be suffering, and she decided to take action on behalf of a neighbor she hadn't even met. "I thought it would be a nice gesture to contact the other neighbors and take up a collection."

Since Ms. Wilburn was unable to do much walking, Calley Wenzel went from door to door, even though it was hard for her to approach strangers and she'd never done anything like that in her life. Still, she put away her fears to help a stranger. Soon she and Ms. Wilburn collected more than six hundred dollars and had offers of furniture, appliances, and clothing.

Ms. Wilburn described what it was like when the strangers at last met: "We called Jimmie and met her at her house. We took her a card signed by all the neighbors. And we gave her the money. She was really surprised. She was amazed at the response of her neighbors."

Jimmie Kincheloe said, "You know how it is today. Nobody has time for anyone. We see each other and wave. But we haven't gotten neighborly. When I moved in, I didn't want to intrude on other people you know are busy. I didn't want to inject myself on them." Now she knows she has some very good neighbors. "A lot of the neighbors felt a real coming together over this. Now they know what they've got, as far as a good neighborhood."

The good deed started by two women has snowballed to fill the block and the hearts of people on it. Said Ms.

Wilburn, "A neighbor two doors away said, 'I wish you'd come around and visit me. I have this lovely deck and I sit here and drink coffee, but I have no one to enjoy it with.' So I'm going to visit."

Having been forced to leave her home while repairs were made, Jimmie Kincheloe said, "I'm anxious to get back home and try being a good neighbor. I can't wait. I'm going to be more caring toward others and more helpful when they need it."

A fire brings neighbors together and goodness produces goodness. That's the power of light over darkness, even in one small neighborhood populated by ordinary people just like us.

Goodness isn't just a state of being; it's a state of doing. It has to be expressed in action to make a difference in this world. If Calley Wenzel or Tossie Wilburn were good people and caring neighbors but never took the risk to act on behalf of Jimmie Kincheloe, the outcome in their neighborhood would have been very different.

It's the same with each of us. We can be the most caring, compassionate people in existence, but the truth will only be told through our actions. We have a choice whether to act or not. Those choices will have an impact on our world.

Making a Bad Choice

I regret to say that I had an opportunity to be a good neighbor, and I blew it. Out on a walk one day, about half a block from home, I saw a little dog trotting out from an open garage door. He tried to follow me down the sidewalk, but I pointed my finger toward his house and said, "Go home." Not knowing much about dogs, I continued my walk, figuring this one would easily find his way back to home and safety. After all, I didn't know those people and didn't even know if I should try to take the dog back. *He looks friendly and cute, but he might bite me,* I reasoned. While I like dogs on principle, I've never fully gotten over a traumatic experience from when I was three and a big, barking dog jumped up on me and ripped the pocket of my jacket. Dogs still make me nervous, and when I pass one on my walk I have to say to myself, "Stay calm. Breathe slowly. They can smell the fear." (I'm sure you dog lovers are laughing at that.)

The next day I saw signs posted with a picture of "Spottie" and guilt began to beat me up badly. Still I couldn't bring myself to show up at the door of those strangers and tell them I'd seen their dog and ignored him. The people sold their home and moved away a few months later, and I don't know if they ever got their dog back. If they did, it was no thanks to me. I chose inaction—and I'll never get a chance to change that decision. I wish I'd taken a risk, gotten over my fear of dogs, and steered little Spottie back home. I hope my failure will motivate me in the future to do the right thing.

When confronted with a choice to act or not to act, we need to stop and consider what Jesus would do in our place. His examples of goodness in action are clear throughout the Gospels—including the one which follows.

The Water
That Quenches Eternally

She sees him sitting by the well, and she slows her steps. Though her water jar is heavy, she is in no hurry to approach a stranger, one who is obviously a Jew and likely to despise a lowly Samaritan woman going about her menial chores in the heat of the midday sun.

Her eyes trace trampled footprints around the well's base as she tries to avoid the stranger's gaze. But she is forced to look up when a voice penetrates her wall of isolation. Surprisingly, the voice is kind, not harsh as she expects.

"Will you give me a drink?"

Her confusion erases thought for a moment. Jews like this man do not associate with Samaritans. She pauses, then casts her eyes to the ground again. "You are a Jew and I am a Samaritan woman. How can you ask me for a drink?"

The man answers, "If you knew the gift of God and who it is that asks you for a drink, you would have asked him and he would have given you living water."

His words are even more baffling than the fact that he addressed her. She replies, "Sir, ... you have nothing to draw with and the well is deep. Where can you get this living water? Are you greater than our father Jacob, who gave us the well and drank from it himself, as did also his sons and his flocks and herds?"

The man answers. "Everyone who drinks this water

will be thirsty again, but whoever drinks the water I give him will never thirst. Indeed, the water I give him will become in him a spring of water welling up to eternal life."

Her heart leaps with an unfamiliar surge of hope. "Sir, give me this water so that I won't get thirsty and have to keep coming here to draw water."

"Go, call your husband and come back."

Now the stranger's words are like a flash of lightning to her soul. "I have no husband," she mumbles.

"You are right when you say you have no husband. The fact is, you have had five husbands, and the man you now have is not your husband. What you have just said is quite true."

The overwhelming truth dawns on her that this is no ordinary conversation, no ordinary Jewish man. She must know more. "Sir, ... I can see that you are a prophet. Our fathers worshiped on this mountain, but you Jews claim that the place where we must worship is in Jerusalem."

His brown eyes lock onto hers. "Believe me, woman, a time is coming when you will worship the Father neither on this mountain nor in Jerusalem. You Samaritans worship what you do not know; we worship what we do know, for salvation is from the Jews. Yet a time is coming and has now come when the true worshipers will worship the Father in spirit and truth, for they are the kind of worshipers the Father seeks. God is spirit, and his worshipers must worship in spirit and in truth."

She responds with what little she has heard. "I know that Messiah ... is coming. When he comes, he will explain everything to us."

The man declares, "I who speak to you am he."

Hope leaps again in her heart, but then she sees a group of men approaching the well. Are they angry with her? It's time to leave. She desperately wants to tell somebody what's happened. There's not even a moment to grab her heavy water jar.

We need to really see those people at our elbows.

Her pounding feet are a herald as she rushes into town and calls to all who might hear. "Come, see a man who told me everything I ever did. Could this be the Christ?" Yet deep inside she knows the answer to her question before anyone can say a word. Indeed, this must be the Christ.

This version taken from John 4:1–29 points out Jesus' goodness in taking a risk and talking with a lowly, degraded woman before he even spoke with the leaders of the little town of Sychar. Imagine how this impoverished, unmarried woman must have felt when she realized that the One who offered her a spring of water welling up to eternal life was the Messiah himself. No doubt she had never before been treated with such respect and concern by someone of high position.

Though he didn't have to, Jesus reached out to the woman at the well. He listened and then gave her what she most needed based on the losses in her life. He recognized her true worth. And in so doing, he provides each of us with a model for showing goodness to others in today's hurting and needy world.

We, too, have a great message about living Water to share with thirsty neighbors and relatives. But we need to pause in the midst of our many activities and busy lives to really see those people at our elbows. We might feel pushed out of our comfort zones sometimes, but it's not necessary to work up a sermon to preach at people. We mostly need to observe and then listen, as Jesus did, so the door can be opened and we might respond with good hearts to meet needs and share truth in the context of loving relationships.

Good deeds must truly be tailored to the needs of others.

A Word of Caution

What we perceive to be good deeds must truly be tailored to the needs of others. It's sometimes too easy to blindly decide what somebody else needs, and then try to shove that good medicine down unwilling throats. This is not unlike my dear, departed great-aunt Frances, as described by my mother in her own words:

Though my mother's sister Frances was seventy-nine years old, she was there for us during Mother's last illness. The family took turns staying up at night in case Mother needed us. Frances volunteered to take the early night shift and stay with Mom until twelve o'clock. We thought that asked too much of her and tried to talk her out of it, but she insisted, and she stayed. Not only that, she came to sit with us during the day too.

During that time she said she didn't believe death was the end. She believed the spirit lived, even though the body died. One day she confided she didn't worry about dying, she worried about not dying. She didn't want to live when she could no longer be useful. When she saw pictures in the paper of a person celebrating his or her hundredth birthday, she'd say, "Oh, what a shame!"

Frances said another thing I'll always remember. She said she'd never had much money, but she'd always had enough. She was rich, though—rich in spirit, rich in her friendships and relationships, and rich in the love she shared with her family.

The time came, though, when, because of dementia, she had to live in a nursing home. While she was there, she kept trying to disconnect another patient's life support equipment. It got so the woman would scream when she saw Frances coming, "Don't let her near me!"

She must have seen Frances as the angel of death, but I feel sure that in Frances' mind, she was trying to do the woman a favor.

My mom, Jane Morton, paints a poignant picture of my great aunt—a woman with a wonderfully good heart, but a woman also determined to do the wrong thing. Dementia had her convinced it was right to disconnect another patient's life support, but that "good deed" existed only in her own mind. Of course, the poor patient and her family saw it from an entirely different perspective.

There have been times when I've taken pride in doing a good work for somebody else, but that action only grew out of my own need. Can you think of an instance like that in your own life? We convince ourselves we're doing it for "their own good," but our efforts don't actually help.

Pharisees were not the examples given us to follow.

Unfortunately, some believers embarrass the rest of us by "doing good" in the name of all of us. But their less-than-loving approach results in more harm than good for the cause of Christ.

I caution myself and anyone else to remember that the Pharisees—those rule-pushers casting judgments—were not the examples given us to follow. Our example is Jesus, with his listening ear and loving heart. He saved his harshest words for the religious leaders of the day, pointing out their unyielding attitudes of self-righteousness.

What Is the True Nature of Goodness?

The secret is following in the steps of the Good Shepherd himself.

When we live in close communion with Jesus, and that relationship is reflected by the Holy Spirit residing in us, we don't have to worry about living good lives. Our lives will naturally display the Spirit inside. The secret is following where he leads, in the steps of the Good Shepherd himself.

And what is the nature of the Good Shepherd? He told us in his own words:

- "He calls his own sheep by name and leads them out. When he has brought out all his own, he goes on ahead of them, and his sheep follow him because they know his voice. But they will never follow a stranger; in fact, they will run away from him because they do not recognize a stranger's voice." (John 10:3–5)

- "I am the gate for the sheep.... Whoever enters though me will be saved. He will come in and go out, and find pasture. The thief comes only to steal and kill and destroy; I have come that they may have life, and have it to the full." (John 10:7, 9–10)

- "I am the good shepherd. The good shepherd lays down his life for the sheep." (John 10:11)
- "I know my sheep and my sheep know me—just as the Father knows me and I know the Father—and I lay down my life for the sheep. I have other sheep that are not of this sheep pen. I must bring them also. They too will listen to my voice, and there shall be one flock and one shepherd. The reason my Father loves me is that I lay down my life—only to take it up again. No one takes it from me, but I lay it down of my own accord." (John 10:14–18)

When we listen to the voice of the Good Shepherd and follow in his way, then we will be able to live out goodness in the world around us. And we can follow the example of Jesus and seek to lay down our lives for others, just as he does for us. Don't we want to be like our Shepherd, as much as we possibly can? Then we need to follow him.

Still, it's important here to be reminded that goodness expressed through action, in other words, "good deeds," will not earn us a pass to heaven. It's always about our relationship with Jesus and trusting in the saving work he performed on the cross:

> Therefore, since we have been justified through faith, we have peace with God through our Lord Jesus Christ, through whom we have gained access by faith into this grace in which we now stand. And we rejoice in the hope of the glory of God. Not only so, but we also rejoice in our sufferings, because

we know that suffering produces perseverance; perseverance, character; and character, hope. And hope does not disappoint us, because God has poured out his love into our hearts by the Holy Spirit, whom he has given us. (Rom. 5:1–5)

So, busy woman, don't just pull out your to-do list and start cataloging all the good things you can think of to help others today. Well, you can do that if you want to, but don't expect checking off that list will bring you closer to the Savior. Instead, take time to open your heart to him and ask the Holy Spirit to direct your actions and draw you closer to the One who "knows everything you ever did."

As the living Water pours from your life, it will naturally nurture those around you.

Goodness in Action

Goodness is not to be confused with niceness.

Goodness is not to be confused with niceness or sweetness. It's not even the same thing as kindness, though expressions of those two fruits of the Spirit can look very similar.

Goodness begins in the heart. Its actions then flow from an attitude of alignment with God's will. A person can be good and still demonstrate that virtue through actions that appear very different from outright kindness—including disciplining or rebuking another person, for instance.

Jesus was good, even when in righteous anger he drove the moneychangers out of the temple. I'm not sure I'd call that an act of kindness, but it certainly reflected his goodness.

Jesus was good, even when in righteous anger he drove out the money-changers.

In the Old Testament, we read about the prophet Nathan—a servant of God who had to firmly confront David, king of Israel. The fruit of Nathan's strength and goodness would change the history of God's people.

King David was a fool for love. Or was it lust? From the moment he caught a glimpse of Bathsheba from the rooftop of the palace, he wanted her. And he took her. Then he had her husband, Uriah, a soldier, transferred to the front lines where the fighting was fiercest. Ultimately, Uriah died and the widow Bathsheba married David and bore him a son. All of this greatly displeased the Lord.

We read this account of what happened next in 2 Samuel 12:1–7:

The LORD sent Nathan to David. When he came
to him, he said, "There were two men in a certain town, one rich and the other poor. The rich
man had a very large number of sheep and cattle, but the poor man had nothing except one
little ewe lamb he had bought. He raised it, and
it grew up with him and his children. It shared
his food, drank from his cup and even slept in
his arms. It was like a daughter to him.

"Now a traveler came to the rich man, but
the rich man refrained from taking one of his
own sheep or cattle to prepare a meal for the
traveler who had come to him. Instead, he took
the ewe lamb that belonged to the poor man and
prepared it for the one who had come to him."

David burned with anger against the man
and said to Nathan, "As surely as the LORD
lives, the man who did this deserves to die! He
must pay for that lamb four times over, because
he did such a thing and had no pity."

Then Nathan said to David, "You are that man!"

Nathan went on to explain that David was like the
rich man in that God had given him everything, but it
was not enough. He had to have Bathsheba too, and he
was willing to take her from another man, even setting
him up for certain death.

David, confronted with his selfish actions, con-
fessed to Nathan, "I have sinned against the LORD."

Nathan replied, "The LORD has taken away your
sin. You are not going to die. But because by doing this
you have made the enemies of the LORD show utter
contempt, the son born to you will die" (vv. 13–14).

Sadly, the consequences of David's sin came to pass. Yet David and Bathsheba would conceive another son, named Solomon, who would grow up to be the wisest man in Israel.

Nathan exhibited goodness in carefully revealing to David the impact of his wrong and selfish choices. He listened to the voice of God and did what he had to do to open up the king's self-deluded eyes. It could not have been an easy conversation, but righteousness demanded that Nathan shed God's light on the darkness that had overtaken David's heart. As one whose life was devoted to serving his Lord, he could do no less.

David's heart, laid bare by the results of his sin, is exposed in the psalms where he confesses his faults and begs God to forgive him:

> Have mercy on me, O God,
>   according to your unfailing love;
>   according to your great compassion
>   blot out my transgressions.
> Wash away all my iniquity
>   and cleanse me from my sin.
> For I know my transgressions,
>   and my sin is always before me.
> Against you, you only, have I sinned
>   and done what is evil in your sight....
> Create in me a pure heart, O God,
>   and renew a steadfast spirit within me.
> Do not cast me from your presence
>   or take your Holy Spirit from me.
> Restore to me the joy of your salvation
>   and grant me a willing spirit, to sustain
>   me.
> (Ps. 51:1–4, 10–12)

The man after God's own heart had failed miserably, and yet he was ultimately restored to a renewed relationship, one that reflected goodness and mercy into the final days of David's life.

Thanks to Nathan's obedience and honest confrontation, David forever exemplifies how the power of a good heart, linked to humility and repentance, can overcome temporary failures and find redemption once again.

Gardener's Tools for Life

Take out your journal, consider these questions, and record your thoughtful answers.

1. If you met Jesus at the well today, and he told you "everything you ever did," what significant life events would be included?
2. What does living water taste like? Describe the effect of living water on your soul.
3. How can you find time to stay close to the Good Shepherd? What changes do you need to make in order to better hear his voice?

Do you have houseplants? Or outdoor plants that need to be watered? If not, buy a small plant for your home or office. Try not to let it die! When you water your houseplants, your garden, or your single, special plant, be reminded of the image of Jesus as living

Water. Think about what the water does for the life of the plant, as it is drawn up through the roots and plumps up the leaves or brightens the blossoms. Take a moment to be thankful for what the living Water is doing in your own life, and let it prompt an outpouring of goodness in a specific way each watering day.

Copy the following passage into your journal and meditate on it this week:

> Grace and peace be yours in abundance through the knowledge of God and of Jesus our Lord.
>
> His divine power has given us everything we need for life and godliness through our knowledge of him who called us by his own glory and goodness. Through these he has given us his very great and precious promises, so that through them you may participate in the divine nature and escape the corruption in the world caused by evil desires.
>
> For this very reason, make every effort to add to your faith goodness; and to goodness, knowledge; and to knowledge, self-control; and to self-control, perseverance; and to perseverance, godliness; and to godliness, brotherly kindness; and to brotherly kindness, love. For if you possess these qualities in increasing measure, they will keep you from being ineffective and unproductive in your knowledge of our Lord Jesus Christ. (2 Peter 1:2–8)

In the weeks to come, try to be aware of instances in your life that present opportunities to

- exercise goodness;
- develop knowledge;
- practice self-control;
- display perseverance;
- offer brotherly kindness;
- demonstrate love.

Be sure to capture those occasions in your journal, so they might encourage you in the future.

Chapter 7

The Fruit of
the Spirit Is ...
Faithfulness

The picture on the front page of our local newspaper catches and holds my attention. It's a picture of an elderly man wearing white trousers, a white shirt, and a safari hat ... and harvesting corn. Bending slightly to place ripe ears of corn into a blue bucket, he is not much taller than the three heavily laden stalks of his crop, aligned next to him like a row of soldiers on parade.

Who is this formally attired farmer? The caption tells me it's ninety-year-old Bill Watson, working in his garden. Though retired for twenty-five years, the veteran of three wars still works in the Bear Creek community garden, taking care of his plot every day from 8 a.m. to 5 p.m., with a lunch break at noon. Not only does he tend his crops there, he also helps gardeners by watering their lots when they're gone on vacation. He has been gardening at the community garden for sixteen years.

Faithfulness means holding yourself accountable to that which you value.

The photo, taken by Jerilee Bennett of the *Gazette*, is arresting. The colors are pretty and the composition striking. But I love its deeper levels of meaning even more than its color and form. If it needed a title, I'd call it "A Portrait of Faithfulness."

Here is a man who could be sitting in an easy chair instead of working in the hot Colorado sun. But he chooses another way to spend his days. Maybe his arthritis acts up occasionally; it's likely his back aches from time to time. But he doesn't let anything stop him. He shows up. He plants and weeds and waters and harvests. He helps his neighbors. Bill Watson is a faithful man. He inspires me, and I have to wonder if I could do half as well, even today.

What does it mean to be faithful—to model faithfulness? It means you stay true, holding yourself accountable to that which you value. You are steadfast and loyal. You keep your promises: to others, to yourself, to God. You do your duty and you are conscientious. You never waver. You are not unlike the Boy Scouts!

The opposite of faithfulness is untrustworthiness, disloyalty, treachery. An unfaithful person cannot be relied upon. An unfaithful spouse is a cheater. An unfaithful soldier is a deserter.

Of course most of us aspire to faithfulness, a key characteristic of our heavenly Father. He is faithful to his own and his love never fails. But the world and our society conspire against our feeble attempts to stay true. Pop culture portrays fickleness as cleverness. In this day and age, getting what you want gets a lot more promotion than doing your duty.

Many of us find it easier to stay faithful in life's major demands. A person shows up at work because the consequences of slacking off can be unemployment. One is faithful to a spouse because love demands it or fear of a broken marriage enforces it. A parent faithfully cares for a child, hoping to raise a fully formed human being who can get a job, move out of the house, and stop leaving those candy wrappers all over the rug.

In my life, I am faithful in many ways. But I realize I'm inclined to prioritize, and there's a definite hierarchy of activities that demand my daily perseverance. That list is often dictated by the severity of what might happen if I don't stay faithful. If I don't brush my teeth, they will fall out (at least that's the threat I use on the kids). If I don't put gas in the car, it won't go, and the car doesn't even care how much I spend to keep it going. If I don't give the cat her asthma inhaler, she'll die.

I admit, there are days when I wonder about the time and money required to keep an asthmatic cat healthy. Never mind my deeper questions about how a cat even has asthma—what is she allergic to herself? Still, every day I call to Sparky, who is an intelligent and generally unobtrusive pet. I say "medicine" and she comes running. I don't think she gets high off the medication or even looks forward to our momentary bonding as I hold her like a baby, look into the dark, liquid pools of her eyes, and squirt the healing mist through a special tube as she breathes for a count of fifteen. She faithfully shows up for her medicine because she has learned that it is followed by a daily dose of tuna. Everybody needs a reward of some kind.

Anyway, a few years ago, Sparky almost expired from an asthma attack, and I do want to keep her around—at least until her owner goes off to college—so I faithfully initiate our routine each morning. We each have our reasons for participating.

But the little things can undo you. Life is complicated and full, and some things are left undone. Dust gathers. Laundry piles up. Paperwork spills out of the in-basket. Friendships are left untended and wither. Prayer time is postponed indefinitely. What was once a vital time of spiritual growth is now just a memory. When faithfulness turns to unfaithfulness, gradual decay sets in.

Eventually, we lose track of little things and they disappear from sight. We don't notice or miss them in our lives. Until we suddenly realize how much of a mess we've made, how far behind we are, how needy we've become. But we need not despair. We can recover from the slide and restore that which is lost. Jesus, our most faithful Friend, sets an unforgettable example of loyalty in his love for others.

A Faithful Friend

Martha pours cool water into a bowl and begins to wash her hands. She used to feel happy at this first step in preparing a meal, but now the routine saddens her, reminding her of the days when mealtime included the three of them: herself, Mary, and Lazarus. Her brother is gone; they would never break bread together again. She can barely believe he has been in the tomb for four days.

The confusion of sudden illness and death, the burial, the many visitors bringing comfort, and a flurry of activity had diverted her thoughts, but now this quiet moment brings grief quickly into her heart. A sob catches in her throat, and tears flow freely.

A sound of pounding feet precedes the knock on the door. "Come! Come out! It's Jesus."

The Rabbi has returned? Her tears cease instantly. She cannot wait to see him. Martha calls out to her sister, working behind the house. "Mary! It's Jesus. Hurry, let's go meet him."

"No!"

Martha is surprised at the anguish in her sister's voice, but she has not a moment to lose. She rushes to greet Jesus, now just a few houses down the road. She struggles to put into words all that she has been feeling for the past week. "Lord, if you had been here, my brother would not have died. But I know that even now God will give you whatever you ask."

Jesus' voice is reassuring. "Your brother will rise again."

"I know he will rise again," says Martha, her words beginning to quaver, "in the resurrection at the last day."

Jesus replies, "I am the resurrection and the life. He who believes in me will live, even though he dies; and whoever lives and believes in me will never die. Do you believe this?"

"Yes, Lord, I believe that you are the Christ, the Son of God, who was to come into the world." It feels so good to put her heartfelt trust into solid words. Wanting to share this hope with her sister, she turns and hurries back to the house to get her.

Other mourners have joined the grieving sisters.

It doesn't take long for all of them to return to Jesus. Mary has run ahead of the group and suddenly she throws herself at his feet, weeping. "Lord, if you had been here, my brother would not have died."

The Rabbi's eyes are filled with tears too. He isn't angry at the sisters' grief-filled accusations. He, too, is weeping. "Where have you laid him?"

"Come and see, Lord." Several in the crowd usher

Jesus toward the tomb, and Martha hurries to keep up. She overhears voices arising here and there: "See how he loved him!"

At last they arrive at the tomb, a cave with a stone laid across the entrance.

"Take away the stone," says Jesus.

Martha is appalled. "But,

We can develop faithfulness as we learn to move ahead in joyful expectation.

Lord, by this time there is a bad odor, for he has been there four days."

Jesus answers, "Did I not tell you that if you believed, you would see the glory of God?"

Martha nods, speechless. A low rumble sounds as four strong men push the stone from its resting place.

"Father," Jesus says, "I thank you that you have heard me. I knew that you always hear me, but I said this for the benefit of the people standing here, that they may believe that you sent me."

A cloak of quiet falls on the bustling crowd, until Jesus' next words crack like lightning: "Lazarus, come out!"

Martha feels as if she cannot breathe or speak. She strains to see the entrance to the cave. Is that a movement in the darkness?

Then a collective gasp goes up as the dead man slowly walks out, his hands and feet wrapped with strips of linen, a cloth around his face.

Jesus directs the stunned crowd. "Take off the grave clothes and let him go."

Martha is the first to run forward, tenderly removing the face cloth. Her brother blinks in the bright sunlight. His eyes shine brightly; he smiles in a way she hasn't seen since he was a little boy.

Incredibly, Lazarus is whole again. Jesus has made it happen. The Lord did not abandon them to their pain and sorrow. She turns to thank Jesus, but he has been swallowed up in a crowd of amazed followers.

As she watches Mary help Lazarus out of his burial clothes, Martha feels certain the time for thank-yous will come. Once again the Lord will grace their table and she, her sister, and her alive-again brother will eat and drink and laugh together, grateful for a second chance because of their ever-faithful friend.

Jesus was faithful to Lazarus, Mary, and Martha, and he is faithful to each of us too. We can trust him to help us and restore our relationship, even during times of great strain.

When Lazarus became ill, the sisters sent word to Jesus, hoping he would hurry to their home and heal their brother. But Jesus delayed, and Lazarus died. For a while Mary wasn't so sure about Jesus' ability or his care, but she and Martha learned again to trust him instead of giving up on him. The tears Jesus wept testified to the depth of his love, and the miracle of resurrection testified to the heights of his power.

Like Mary and Martha, we can develop the fruit of faithfulness as we deepen our trust and learn to move ahead in joyful expectation instead of anxiety and dread. The ultimate resurrection awaits all who follow, after all. (Taken from John 11:17–44.)

Real-World Faithfulness

Marriage can offer one of the best arenas for examples of real-world faithfulness. My parents have been married more than fifty years, and many of their friends' marriages have endured just as long. Mom offered me this story of faithful friends in a difficult time:

> My husband, Dick, was ill with what turned out to be leukemia, but at the time we were still awaiting a diagnosis. He'd lost his appetite, and he wasn't sleeping. The worst of it all was not knowing what caused his symptoms.
>
> Aware of our situation, my friend Rusty called to tell us she and her husband, Ron, would pick us up the next morning and take us to breakfast, not at a restaurant, but at a park. They would bring the food and cook it for us.
>
> We welcomed the opportunity to get away from our problems for a short time, to be outdoors in the warm sunshine, and to enjoy the comfort and support of good friends. Dick's health was on all of our minds, but his illness and their kindness created a special bond between us.

I'll never forget sitting in the shade of the mesquite trees, under the clear blue sky, watching the birds circling above us. I had been reading the book *Message on the Wind* by Clay Jenkinson. In it he asks, "If your spirit could return to earth, where would you have it go?" The question called to mind places we had been, and places on earth that meant the most to us. Ron touched me with his answer, "I'd want to go with Rusty."

It would be months before we could do anything that special again. As Dick went through treatment, we often talked about Rusty and Ron and their love that helped see us through this difficult time.

> *Hard times can spur us on to greater levels of faithfulness.*

Hard times can cause us to falter in our faithfulness, or they can spur us on to greater levels of faithfulness.

But even in easier times, it can be difficult in our fast-paced lives to stay true and answer the calling God has for us. I want to make excuses for my many failings in the area of faithfulness:

- Nobody knows the workload I've seen.
- The kids' schedules are driving my life.
- I'm behind on umpteen deadlines.
- I can't get any help around here.

- The weather is giving me a sinus headache.
- I'm too tired to do anything but watch TV.
- I can't volunteer because I'm busy, busy, busy.

Recent magazine articles have instructed overtaxed readers to "learn to say 'no.'" Trust me. I've mastered "no" and a whole lot more. What I need is a lesson in enlarging my heart so that when the time is right I'm ready to say "yes."

Like the Chicken Man. His real name was Albert Wallace and he passed away a few weeks before I wrote this. The disabled, alcoholic Vietnam veteran ended up homeless in 1980 before turning his life around. In the eleven years before his death he operated the GoodNews Foundation, giving food, clothes, cash, and other items to our city's poor.

Over the years, Chicken Man earned his nickname for taking buckets of fried chicken to the Red Cross homeless shelter on Sundays. At Thanksgiving and Christmas, he made gift baskets and lined up volunteers to cook turkey dinners. Through his foundation, thousands of children received free vision tests and glasses, and hundreds were sent to summer camp. He helped people with rent and utility bills, sometimes giving away the last few dollars in his pocket.

Albert Wallace wasn't rich. He wasn't famous. But he was faithful. He told the local newspaper, "Working for the Lord doesn't pay much, but the retirement plan is the greatest on earth."

If the Chicken Man could find a way to make a difference, then I can too. So can you.

My friend Lisa began a quilting ministry at her church. She's passionate about quilting, so she's leading a group of women in making beautiful quilts to give to foster children and people in their church going through loss and difficult times. Lisa says, "God put this on my heart, and I had no idea what he was going to do with it. But I had to do my part." A busy mom with her own business, Lisa's employing her unique gifts and interests to change lives for the better. Maybe she'll let me call her the Quilt Lady. Like the Chicken Man, she's blooming *before* she's planted and bearing the sweet fruit of faithfulness.

> *Our faith is demonstrated in physical ways.*

Do you know anybody like the Chicken Man or the Quilt Lady—someone who has been faithful to you or others in your world? Consider whether that person has had a wealth of extra time, money, and energy. Or is that person just an ordinary anybody with an extraordinary faith?

What about you? Do you feel the Spirit prompting you to take inventory of your skills and the needs around you? If a bell goes off in your heart, will you answer the call to serve? Do you trust God to equip you with the energy and time you need to reach out to the world around you? Look to faithfulness in the small things, and it will lead to a life that has the power to make big things happen.

It's true that our efforts won't buy us a front-row seat in heaven. But our faith is demonstrated in physical ways, in the real world, and it shouts its presence to others. A passage in the book of James is fairly adamant on this point:

> What good is it, my brothers, if a man claims to have faith but has no deeds? Can such faith save him? Suppose a brother or sister is without clothes and daily food. If one of you says to him, "Go, I wish you well; keep warm and well fed," but does nothing about his physical needs, what good is it? In the same way, faith by itself, if it is not accompanied by action, is dead.
>
> But someone will say, "You have faith; I have deeds."
>
> Show me your faith without deeds, and I will show you my faith by what I do....
>
> As the body without the spirit is dead, so faith without deeds is dead. (James 2:14–18, 26)

Faithfulness in Action

While many men and women of God portrayed in Scripture demonstrated faithfulness, the apostle Paul lived what he wrote in the epistles, overcoming obstacles and hardships in order to spread the good news of Jesus Christ.

In the course of his travels, Paul endured difficult journeys, bad health, shipwrecks, beatings, and persecution. He was placed under house arrest in Rome where he awaited trial on an appeal to the Roman emperor Nero. During this period of incarceration, he wrote to the believers at Philippi. In spite of all he had been through, Paul's words reflect his incredible spirit of faithfulness and encouragement to others. Here are a few excerpts of this letter, which demonstrate faithfulness in action:

- I have you in my heart; for whether I am in chains or defending and confirming the gospel, all of you share in God's grace with me. God can testify how I long for all of you with the affection of Christ Jesus. (Phil. 1:7–8)

- What has happened to me has really served to advance the gospel. As a result, it has become clear throughout the whole palace guard and to everyone else that I am in chains for Christ. Because of my chains, most of the brothers in the Lord have been encouraged to speak the word of God more courageously and fearlessly. (Phil. 1:12–14)

- I will continue to rejoice, for I know that through your prayers and the help given by the Spirit of Jesus Christ, what has happened to me will turn out for my deliverance. (Phil. 1:18–19)

- For to me, to live is Christ and to die is gain. If I am to go on living in the body, this will mean fruitful labor for me. Yet what shall I choose? I do not know! I am torn between the two: I desire to depart and be with Christ, which is better by far; but it is more necessary for you that I remain in the body. Convinced of this, I know that I will remain, and I will continue with all of you for your progress and joy in the faith. (Phil. 1:21–25)

- Even if I am being poured out like a drink offering on the sacrifice and service coming from your faith, I am glad and rejoice with all of you. So you too should be glad and rejoice with me. (Phil. 2:17–18)
- I know what it is to be in need, and I know what it is to have plenty. I have learned the secret of being content in any and every situation, whether well fed or hungry, whether living in plenty or in want. I can do everything through him who gives me strength. (Phil. 4:12–13)

These passages reveal the heart of a man sold out to God, who does not live in regret for the pain and deprivation he has gone through, but who looks forward to completing his work. Indeed, his teaching and writing continued until the end of his life, in spite of incredible challenges.

The apostle Paul himself anticipated his future near the end of his life, when his own faithfulness—in the face of tremendous obstacles—would be rewarded. "I have fought the good fight, I have finished the race, I have kept the faith. Now there is in store for me the crown of righteousness, which the Lord, the righteous Judge, will award to me on that day—and not only to me, but also to all who have longed for his appearing" (2 Tim. 4:7–8).

Paul is a tremendous model of a life of faithfulness maintained throughout trials and testing—a man who, in spite of everything, still held onto an attitude of joy embedded in the very foundation of his soul.

Gardener's Tools for Life

Consider the Lord's faithfulness to you today and throughout your life. Perhaps your thoughts may be inspired by that classic hymn, "Great Is Thy Faithfulness." See the example in Nancy's story at the end of this chapter, then start a page in your journal where you list all the ways in which God has shown his faithfulness to you.

After that, start another page in your journal and title it, "Great Is *My* Faithfulness." List all the areas of your life where you already exhibit faithfulness, small and large. Write down daily obligations and regular tasks. Then describe broader areas of faithfulness: in relationships and responsibilities, in years past and in years ahead. List any dreams you may have for expressing your love for God through ministry. Create a plan for turning that ministry into a reality.

The Israelites developed concrete ways to remind themselves about God's faithfulness to them. They followed the instruction of God's Word, which told them, "Love the LORD your God with all your heart and with all your soul and with all your strength. These commandments that I give you today are to be upon your hearts. Impress them on your children. Talk about them when you sit at home and when you walk along the road, when you lie down and when you get up. Tie them as symbols on your hands and bind them on your foreheads. Write them on the doorframes of your houses and on your gates" (Deut. 6:5–9).

Do you have a small item, perhaps a favorite piece of jewelry, that can serve as your symbol of God's faithfulness to you and your love for him? Designate a sign to serve as a specific reminder each day. If not jewelry, it could be a permanent part of your home that you naturally look at each day—a picture on the wall, a magnet on the refrigerator, that cobweb in the corner. You don't have to bind your reminder to your forehead, but you should see it daily and think of your relationship with the One who made you.

Fruit trees can exemplify faithfulness as they present us with their gifts year after year. Read the following poem, written by my mother, Jane Ambrose Morton. Then write your thoughts about it in your journal:

THE APRICOT TREE

Far out on the plains in the wind and the dust
Lived an apricot tree that survived what it must.

That tree wasn't pampered. That tree
       wasn't pruned.
When wind broke a branch, no one doctored
       the wound.

Though weakened by insects, harsh
    weather and drought,
Spring after spring that tree would leaf out.

Some years it had cots; some years it did not.
The fruit was quite small, but much
    sweeter than bought.

It went without water. It went without care.
But thirty years later that tree was still there.

One winter the tree finally died of old age.
The skeleton overlooks yucca and sage.

It stands as a symbol of struggle and grit,
Of those who keep going when tempted to
    quit.

The settler who planted it wasn't around,
But the apricot tree had proved up on that
    ground.

So how did that tree live three decades or
    more?
Could it be that adversities strengthened
    its core?

Read these words from Scripture and let them live
before you in the week to come. Tuck them into your
heart before you go to sleep at night.

Know therefore that the Lord your God is God;
he is the faithful God, keeping his covenant of
love to a thousand generations of those who love
him and keep his commands. (Deut. 7:9)

> The LORD is gracious and righteous;
> our God is full of compassion.
> The LORD protects the simplehearted;
> when I was in great need, he
> saved me.
> Be at rest once more, O my soul,
> for the LORD has been good to you.
> For you, O LORD, have delivered my soul
> from death,
> my eyes from tears,
> my feet from stumbling,
> that I may walk before the LORD
> in the land of the living.
> (Ps. 116:5–9)

> Let love and faithfulness never leave you;
> bind them around your neck
> write them on the tablet of your heart.
> (Prov. 3:3)

After you read the following story, start a page in
your journal and list several instances when God has
been faithful to you.

NANCY'S STORY

One morning in December I came home from the grocery store with a perfectly lovely pink poinsettia. I placed it in a ceramic pot and set it in the middle of the coffee table in my living room. All day I admired it as I bustled about with my holiday preparations. But when it came time for me to leave to meet with the single mom I mentor in Bible study, the Spirit nudged me to take the poinsettia as a gift for her. I tried to avoid the nudging because it looked so nice in my living room. But I also knew it would totally transform the tiny apartment in which my friend lived. Somewhat reluctantly, I grabbed the poinsettia and off I went. My friend's total delight let me know I'd made the right choice.

That evening, imagine my surprise when I opened the door to one of my Bible study friends and could barely see the top of her head behind the huge, pink poinsettia plant she was carrying. "Something told me you might like this," she said, as she handed me the plant that was twice the size of the one I had given away. God is so good. When we allow him to influence us to do even the smallest act of giving, he's very likely to shower us with his gifts.

Chapter 8

The Fruit of the Spirit Is ...

Gentleness

What does gentleness look like? To some it appears in the form of a delicate rose petal. To others it may be pictured as one hand tenderly holding another. To me, at one time, the word *gentleness* would have instantly evoked a mental image of a mother cradling a newborn infant.

Of course, that was before I had a couple of infants of my own. All at one time. Anticipated hours in a rocking chair singing sweet lullabies were, in reality, spent juggling diaper changes, baths, and the inevitable multiple feeding times. And speaking of feeding, nursing twins was anything but a gentle act as those hungry mouths clamped down on my tender flesh to enjoy a nice, long drink while I winced in toe-curling pain.

Yes, cultural images of motherhood often portray the gentle side, but moms in the trenches have learned the truth: You have to be tough to be tender.

But tenderness doesn't always come naturally to humans. I remember trying to teach my rambunctious boys the concept of a gentle touch. With rough-and-tumble toddlers like my own, this is a foreign idea. Try as I might to civilize them, they acted more like puppies or untrained chimps in those early years. Of course, in those days, once they discovered the pleasures of hitting each other, our concept of gentleness was reduced to "no hitting" and "no biting."

I learned to guard my precious possessions. Not the furniture or breakables; those things were goners anyway. I mostly wanted to teach my boys to handle books carefully and gently. They got pretty good at turning pages without ripping them, and I even let them handle my Bible once in a while. I'd pull it off the shelf, and let them feel its leathery cover. "Bible," I would croon, while guiding a chubby hand to carefully stroke the outside. "God's book. Be gentle."

> *You have to be tough to be tender.*

I was pleased that my boys were getting the idea as they grew and learned to talk. "Bible," one would say, as he tapped my Bible's cover.

"Yes," I'd assure him. "God's special book, the Bible."

Then I discovered I'd misled them slightly. Chris had pulled my checkbook, with its fake leather cover, from my purse. He touched it and held it up to me. Obviously it felt special, like something he'd touched before. "Bible," he stated.

As my boys grew, it became clear they weren't lap children. They were happy with a minimum of hugs and kisses. I'd pull them to me for a squeeze or to sit on my lap, and

Gentleness is not a trait much touted in our me-first, modern-day society.

they'd wriggle away. They were high-action kids from the beginning and still are today. They'd wrestle and roll around, race each other, and crash their toy cars. But they seldom exhibited a gentle touch or a quiet moment, unless sound asleep.

The cats finally brought out the gentle side of my guys. One year, on their birthday, Chris was given Sparky. Things changed then. The twins both lavished love on the little gray cat, and two years later showered their affection also on Yoda, Jon's tiger-striped kitty plucked from the animal shelter.

Now I often see one of my boys, face buried in cat fur, talking in a soft voice and handling with care. The cats have taught these boys the art of gentleness in a way I never could. I can model these characteristics, but the cats provide a way to practice them. While gentle actions may not have come naturally to my boys, they have learned to be gentle and express their love appropriately to their pets. I guess that makes it worth all the scratches on the woodwork and rips in the rugs.

> *Which of our celebrated athletes is known for his or her tender heart?*

Gentleness is, of course, one of the nine character traits listed as fruit of the Spirit. It is not a trait much touted in our me-first, modern-day society. When's the last time somebody won a season of *Survivor* by virtue of his or her gentleness? Which of our celebrated athletes is known for his or her tender heart and gentle spirits? How many leaders climbed to the tops of corporate ladders thanks to gentleness? A few, perhaps. But I can't easily think of any, can you?

Jesus was a gentle man. He said so himself: "Take my yoke upon you and learn from me, for I am gentle and humble in heart, and you will find rest for your souls" (Matt. 11:29). Imagine what it would have been like to encounter the gentleness of Jesus just when you needed it most.

A Gentle Strength

She knows she is going to die. And she has no excuse. What she did was wrong—against the law—and the price will be her life. The boiling crowd of teachers and Pharisees that bully and push her along the road will see that she is punished, stoned to death in plain view of her tormentors.

But her total humiliation must come first, worse than death itself, which at least will give her relief from her shame.

Where are they taking me? Dust, flailing arms, and the din of shouted curses dampen her sense of time and place. Then through the haze of fear she knows where she is. The temple.

The surrounding crowd splits apart and she is pulled into a clearing. She sees the one they call Jesus.

A red-faced Pharisee, breathing heavily, spits out his words. "Teacher, this woman was caught in the act of adultery. In the Law Moses commanded us to stone such women. Now what do you say?"

Jesus looks in her direction and she averts her eyes. Through lowered lashes she sees him crouch down and write on the ground with his finger.

The impatient Pharisees hurl their questions like weapons in a battle. "Shall we stone her now?" "Do you defy the Law of Moses?" "Answer us! Why don't you speak?"

At last, the questioners fall silent.

Jesus stands up straight and quietly says, "If any one of you is without sin, let him be the first to throw a stone at her."

Again he stoops down and writes on the ground. She wants to look away in her shame, but finds she cannot tear her eyes away from him.

She steels her body for the first blow of a stone. Yet she feels nothing. As she watches Jesus, she hears the sounds of footsteps behind her, shuffling, becoming more distant. Murmurs accompany the footfalls, until they too fade away. At last it is completely quiet.

Jesus stands again and walks closer. "Woman, where are they? Has no one condemned you?"

She dares to turn around and sees that the temple courtyard is completely deserted. "No one, sir," she stammers her astonished answer.

"Then neither do I condemn you," Jesus declares. "Go now and leave your life of sin."

She bows her head and turns to go. Deep inside she discovers a feeling she has not known for many years. Warmth rises to fill her soul: It is the sweet promise of hope.

Jesus showed great gentleness to the woman caught in the act of adultery (see John 8:1–11). But he also revealed great strength. He stood up to the woman's accusers and refused to let them judge her unfairly. That act of protection reflected his teaching during the Sermon on the Mount:

"Do not judge, or you too will be judged. For in the same way you judge others, you will be judged, and with the measure you use, it will be measured to you.

"Why do you look at the speck of sawdust in your brother's eye and pay no attention to the plank in your own eye? How can you say to your brother, 'Let me take the speck out of your eye,' when all the time there is a plank in your own eye? You hypocrite, first take the plank out of your own eye, and then you will see clearly to remove the speck from your brother's eye." (Matt. 7:1–5)

Refusing to forgive others means we have not caught the message of grace.

The Lord treated the woman as he also treats us, with grace and love. While he has every right to throw stones at us, because he was totally without blame, he grants us mercy and withholds judgment. And he expects us to treat others in the way he has treated us.

Gentleness can more easily flow out of our lives when we fully understand the way we have been pardoned. We do not deserve to be forgiven, yet we have been. Refusing to forgive others and treating them harshly, even for real wrongs they have committed, means we have not caught the message of grace taught in the life of Christ. He has saved us so that we can be instrumental in saving others.

A Story of Gentleness

My friend Ben is tall and strong. He's a big guy who sports a shaved head and a fish tattoo on one ear. He's also got an incredibly gentle spirit. His physical strength is sometimes tested by the fact that he has an artificial leg, but as a former high school athlete, he still manages to convey power in the way he moves and confidence in the way he smiles. Having won his battle with cancer in his teen years, Ben is now an adult with an inner strength stemming from reliance on God.

To me, Ben is a model of the fruit of the Spirit, but especially in the area of gentleness. Recently, he put that gentleness to work helping two men in Boquillas, Mexico. Here's an excerpt from the letter he sent to those who helped support his efforts:

> Donato (the team leader) and I went to Boquillas in February to outfit Antonio with his new prosthetic leg. What I found out was that his need was more intense than originally thought. Antonio became an amputee much like me though cancer. He had two very well used and broken wooden legs that were moldy and no longer fit his remaining leg. He still has his knee which really helps in creating a prosthesis and cuts down on the overall cost. He also had a knee brace on his remaining leg supported with metal bars which act like a brace but give no actual support to the knee. I thought Antonio was about fifty years old, but he was actually over seventy. He sure didn't have that appearance; he was youthful in spirit and in his face.
>
> Alfredo's need for the wheelchair was no less important. We came to find out that he was closer to a sixteen-year-old with many medical conditions that made him a paraplegic. Another church in the U.S. had heard about him and sent a hospital wheelchair in December last year. When Donato and I looked at it, it had already begun to break apart. By taking Alfredo his new Quickie wheelchair with Mag wheels and mountain bike tires, he is now able to travel the rocky terrain of this small town.
>
> With the help of a local prosthetic company, we were able to make Antonio a new leg.

That alone was worth the trip to see the excitement in his face. Antonio looked like a young boy at Christmas time opening a brand new gift. He was so appreciative and excited, I wish each of you could have seen his expression.

Alfredo received even more gifts from the high school students that participated in a fund-raiser for the wheelchair and other supplies. He was elated at the gifts and the newfound mobility with his Quickie.

I couldn't go anywhere where there are children without playing with Legos. I had this privilege as well during the Youth Rally presented by our students. Legos helped me connect to the local children where communication couldn't. We just had a great time being kids.

When I first went to Boquillas in February, a young boy named Roberto came up to me and just wanted to be friends. He didn't care about my leg (I wore shorts both times I was there) or that I couldn't speak a word of Spanish. But I had my digital camera and was able to show pictures to try and communicate. That worked wonderfully. Berto, as we called him, received a Lego gift too. I made it a special project that week to spend some extra time building a toy while building a relationship.

Gentleness is two-sided, and its flip side is strength.

Your heart helped in my discovery of this type of relationship. Your heart provided the means to financially go and prayerfully succeed. You may never fully know the blessings that were planted on this trip, but I thank you for the privilege to represent you as the

Gentleness requires us to withhold our strength.

"Hands and Heart of Jesus." I am grateful for all that was provided and thank the Lord for everything accomplished.

The last line of the passage above sums it up: "I can do everything through him who gives me strength." Without Jesus, everything is in vain; with Jesus everything can be done.

That's my friend Ben. He really illustrates that gentleness is two-sided, and its flip side is strength. I love the photo he sent, a grown-up among little kids, playing Legos and sharing the love of Jesus.

Gentle People in a Me-First World

When do you find it hardest to be gentle? When you're in a hurry and something or someone is getting in your way? When you're generally frustrated by life and its inability to bend to your convenience? How about when you're driving on the highway or else when a child or your boss seems bent on driving you crazy?

Aggressiveness is actually fear in disguise.

It's easy to be gentle when the soft music plays and a quiet breeze cools your brow. Its not easy to express gentleness 99 percent of the rest of the time when real life pummels your expectations into the ground.

What can help? For me, taking a deep breath and a moment to get some perspective helps. Instead of snapping at work and letting somebody have a piece of my mind, I need to mentally relax and remember that my own life has no doubt interfered with somebody else's. Or recall those timeless words from Proverbs 15:1, "A gentle answer turns away wrath, but a harsh word stirs up anger."

Gentleness requires us to withhold our strength. I learned that meaning while trying to teach my little boys to touch the Bible carefully. Don't grab. Don't pull. We don't rush; we don't force. We hold back and move slowly. And we don't hit either—even if your brother seems to deserve it.

I need to learn to lead with my heart and not my tongue, to listen and not judge. I have to turn my personality over to Jesus and ask him to perform an extreme, complete home makeover on my selfish self. I can't just summon up a glass of gentleness. I need to continually drink from the living Water so that his way will pour forth from my life.

What will aid me in this? Studying the Gospels helps, because the accounts in Matthew, Mark, Luke, and John remind me that Jesus is always the best teacher. His examples inspire me and the Holy Spirit enables me to grow into the woman he wants me to be—even at my advanced, middle age.

The Soul Whisperer

A few years ago I saw a movie based on a book called *The Horse Whisperer*. The story involves a horse that has been horribly traumatized—mentally and physically—because of a near-fatal accident with a truck. Once a beloved pet, it becomes fearful and wild. So its owners take it to be treated by a man famous for his ability to gentle horses. The horse whisperer's patience and care eventually restore the animal to its full potential, where it can trust people and be loved once again.

In many ways, we are like that horse. We have been hurt by the world. Our anxiety and fearfulness stirs up the adrenaline in our bodies, and that constant stress pushes us to run from danger or else fight back furiously.

Along comes Jesus, our Soul Whisperer. He is quiet and strong and stays with us, despite our injuries. He begins to calm our hearts, and before long we learn to understand what he is telling us. When we settle down and listen to his voice, we feel deeply cared for and our hearts open up to the gentleness he offers. Gentleness begets gentleness and we begin to heal. Soon we can respond to others, even the most obnoxious among us, with a gentle manner and a soothed spirit.

The opposite of gentleness is assertiveness and, ultimately, aggressiveness. The world often applauds that behavior and rewards the aggressive with better-paying jobs and higher esteem. But aggressiveness is actually fear in disguise. Fighting to be first assures us we won't be left behind, that we'll get other people before they get us.

Gentleness stems from confidence that the Lord will meet our needs, whether we are first in line or at the very end. It is grounded in strength, not weakness, and it leads us to true peace.

Gentleness in Action

When I think of strength submitted in service to God, the person described in the Bible who first comes to mind is Mary, mother of Jesus.

This young woman from a small town found herself

suddenly visited by the angel Gabriel. Of course, this surprise was both frightening and astounding. His promises were amazing: "You have found favor with God. You will be with child and give birth to a son, and you are to give him the name Jesus. He will be great and will be called the Son of the Most High. The Lord God will give him the throne of his father David, and he will reign over the house of Jacob forever; his kingdom will never end." (See Luke 1:26–38.)

Mary was young and innocent, yet her faith was mature. She answered, simply, "I am the Lord's servant.... May it be to me as you have said." Yet little did she know the sacrifices she would be required to make in the decades to come.

Mary's humble feelings about God's calling are recorded in a passage known as "Mary's Song," Luke 1:46–55:

> My soul praises the Lord
> and my spirit rejoices in God my Savior,
> for he has been mindful
> of the humble state of his servant.
> From now on all generations will call me blessed,
> for the Mighty One has done
> great things for me—
> holy is his name.
> His mercy extends to those who fear him,
> from generation to generation.
> He has performed mighty deeds with his arm;
> he has scattered those who are proud in
> their inmost thoughts.
> He has brought down rulers from their thrones
> but has lifted up the humble.

> He has filled the hungry with good things
>> but has sent the rich away empty.
> He has helped his servant Israel,
>> remembering to be merciful
> to Abraham and his descendants forever,
>> even as he said to our fathers.

With such a position of prominence, such an important role to fulfill, Mary could have grown proud—asserting herself as a diva instead of submitting to play the part of a humble servant. Instead we see her pictured throughout history as the Madonna, the gentle mother of the Christ child.

Mary was fully aware of her humble status, a status that never really changed throughout her life. She would bear a son, carefully and gently tend him as an infant and young child, and then draw upon every bit of strength she had in order to fulfill her role as the mother of the Messiah. She would listen to his teaching and watch him heal the sick and injured. She would endure uncertainty and pain, and she would at last watch her beloved son hang on a wooden cross.

Mary would find a new role as Jesus entrusted her to the care of his beloved disciple John, a gesture made in his dying moments. "Dear woman," he said, "here is your son." And to John, "Here is your mother." (See John 19:26–27.)

Mary's inner strength would be tested in every way, but in the end, her grief would turn to joy at the resurrection of Christ. This humble, gentle woman had raised the Son of God, and he, in turn, would become her own Savior—and the Savior of the world.

Gardener's Tools for Life

Fruit is a sweet metaphor, isn't it? While it's a bit of a stretch to think of fruit itself as gentle, the scent of most fruit usually is a gentle scent. And fruit blossoms? Don't even get me started!

Today, why don't you find yourself a piece of fruit as a snack or dessert, and before you eat it, pause and take in its aroma?

While you enjoy the fragrance of your chosen piece of fruit, close your eyes and contemplate the nature of gentleness. What pictures come to mind when you consider the word *gentleness?* Fix an image in your mind and, after you eat that fruit, write a paragraph in your journal comparing Jesus' example of gentleness with the image you pictured.

Do you know somebody who, like my friend Ben, is strong yet gentle? What is it about that person's life that communicates gentleness? How do other people respond to that person? Write your ideas in your journal.

As our family cats brought out the gentleness in my rough-and-tumble twins, there may be people or pets that bring out the gentle touch in you. Make a list of possibilities. As you encounter the items on your list, consider how much more gently God treats us in his love and forgiveness. Take time to thank him for his gentle care.

Answer these questions in your journal: What was the last time I neglected to show gentleness to somebody who needed it? What prevented me from being gentle in my behavior or my speech? How can I better lean on Jesus when the next occasion arises?

Take time this week to consider and study these passages of scripture and words from a beautiful hymn that remind us of the grace we have been granted, even in dark times. Can your prayer this week be, "Lord, lead me on"?

Your beauty should not come from outward adornment, such as braided hair and the wearing of gold jewelry and fine clothes. Instead, it should be that of your inner self, the unfading beauty of a gentle and quiet spirit, which is of great worth in God's sight. (1 Peter 3:3–4)

Remember this: Whoever sows sparingly will also reap sparingly, and whoever sows generously will also reap generously. Each man should give what he has decided in his heart to give, not reluctantly or under compulsion, for God loves a cheerful giver. And God is able to make all grace abound to you, so that in all things at all times, having all that you need, you will abound in every good work. (2 Cor. 9:6–8)

I know what it is to be in need, and I know what it is to have plenty. I have learned the secret of being content in any and every situation, whether well fed or hungry, whether living in plenty or in want. I can do everything through him who gives me strength. (Phil. 4:12–13)

LEAD, KINDLY LIGHT
John H. Newman

Lead, kindly Light, amid th' encircling
    gloom, lead Thou me on!
The night is dark, and I am far from home;
    lead Thou me on!
Keep Thou my feet; I do not ask to see
The distant scene; one step enough for me.

I was not ever thus, nor prayed that Thou
    shouldst lead me on;
I loved to choose and see my path; but now
    lead Thou me on!
I loved the garish day, and, spite of fears,
Pride ruled my will. Remember not past years!

So long Thy power hath blest me, sure it still
    will lead me on.
O'er moor and fen, o'er crag and torrent, till
    the night is gone,
And with the morn those angel faces smile,
    which I
Have loved long since, and lost awhile!

Chapter 9

The Fruit of the Spirit Is ...

Self-control

I started my diet again today. This is unusual for me because I almost always start my diets on a Monday and today is a Wednesday. So I'm two days late. Actually, two days and about six months late if I really want to lose those fifteen pounds before my reunion in a week and a half. I'm pretty sure, even if I do a great job, I won't be shedding fifteen pounds in ten and a half days. The numbers just don't work out. But at least now I'm motivated by the urgency. If only I could demonstrate such self-control when my deadline is further away, I might have a chance of achieving my goal.

At this point, I'm looking for shortcuts to success. Maybe I should go on the high-protein diet again. Last time I tried that, it worked a little bit. Well, I lost five pounds overnight, and then I never lost another ounce in the four months I managed to live without the carbs I crave daily. Still, I'd be glad to lose even five pounds, just to get me through the reunion, and then I'll revert to my happy, high-carb lifestyle.

Self-control seems foundational to a fruit-bearing life.

Surely there's a pill that can help me? I'll run over to my local drugstore later today and see what's new. The promises on the packaging always give me a little thrill, not to mention those amazing before-and-after pictures of people who used the products.

Wait, what's this? Here's an old e-mail I printed out before our spam protector put an end to weight-loss pitches, among other blatant sales ploys. I guess I saved it because I thought it was funny—its clumsy wording and the fact that it's addressed to some person who not only doesn't live here, but who probably doesn't even exist. Still, I'm getting desperate, so maybe I should read it again. Who knows? It could be legitimate. The company might still be in business. Weight-loss miracles can happen.

> Subject: Timely direction for ridding mass!
> From: Portia Nein
> Date: 30 Dec 2005
> To: Clifford Fbolp
>   Our tablets is an innovative fat-bonding supplement which removes fat from a fare you gobble! Contrived with the potent grease-bandage filament, the mixture of all-natural compounds....
>
> Control this

Sadly, I didn't print out the entire message, and it ends abruptly with some computer-generated demand that I "control this." I wish I were a good example of self-control, but my efforts to whittle this middle-aged waistline prove that I'm not. Only recently (probably on a Monday when I was starting my diet, again) did I "discover" the incredible concept that in order to work, diets generally have to be adhered to every single day. One of my biggest downfalls is that I really prefer the day before the diet starts. Those are the best days ever! You can eat what you want, without guilt, because tomorrow is the day the diet starts. But if you never actually get to the day the diet starts, it's a whole lot harder to lose weight.

Since I'm putting it all out there on the table (in more ways than one), I admit that, of all the fruit of the Spirit, self-control is the very hardest for me to exhibit consistently. And not just in the area of sticking to my diet, but in many aspects of life. I suspect that may be true for you too. Yielding to temptation has been a problem for humans like us ever since Eve first took a bite of that apple, kumquat, or whatever forbidden fruit it was that tasted too good to be true.

A Bit of Pruning

In many ways, self-control seems foundational to a fruit-bearing life. I can't imagine being able to experience and display love, joy, peace, patience, kindness, goodness, faithfulness, and gentleness, if I had no self-control. Because ultimately my self-control will fail, I'm actually hoping to live a life that is Spirit-controlled. That means submission is the key to a life that reflects the character of Jesus to this hurting world.

God helps us delay gratification so that we can taste the best that life has.

What does submission look like? It's setting aside my selfish urges and asking the Lord to help me show restraint regarding my impulses, emotions, and desires. It looks a lot like pruning—and I'm the plant, not the gardener.

When my husband and I bought our first little house in Illinois, we were excited new homeowners. With no kids or pets to care for, I felt the need to nurture something, and the corner lot offered a great chunk of abandoned garden, a square of dirt just begging to be planted. So I ordered gardening catalogs and got inspired to plant strawberries. When my fifty rooted seedlings arrived, I went to work. I tilled the soil, dug holes, and added fertilizer. I tenderly ensconced each green seedling in its cradle of rich earth. I weeded and watered.

I dreamed about my crop-to-be and pictured myself harvesting berries for breakfast in a few months.

Then I talked with a friend who had actually grown strawberries of her own.

"You know you have to pick off all the blossoms this year," she informed me.

"What? But doesn't that mean I won't get any strawberries?"

"Right. You have to prune them this year and prevent them from bearing fruit. That way the plants will be stronger and the berries bigger in the years that follow. Otherwise you'll just have sour berries and weak plants. Just pinch off all the blossoms."

My friend's advice was pretty hard to take. I wanted my strawberries that summer, not a year later, especially after all my hard work. But I gritted my teeth and plucked those delicate, white blossoms, and in many years that followed I enjoyed delicious, sweet berries from my own garden. The sacrifice was well worth it.

The pruning of our own desires is something like that. God helps us delay gratification or give up something we really want, so that we can taste the best that life has in store for us a little later. We could give in to the temptation of grabbing at our present desires, but we would miss the sweeter, more abundant harvest that awaits.

In the life of Christ, self-control and resisting temptation were issues that arose very early in his ministry. Though he was fully God, it wasn't a simple thing to stand up to the ultimate temptation. Especially when he was also fully man, and a hungry man at that.

Let's take a look at the account in Matthew 4:1–11 and consider it from a supernatural point of view.

A Battle Is Won

Michael knows something about the art of war. As Archangel, he is the leader of the Lord's forces in the constant battle against the Evil One. He knows that wars are not won on the battlefield, but within hearts. Today he wishes he could see into the heart of Jesus, for a fierce struggle is underway in the desert. He cannot turn his eyes from the scene, but he cannot interfere.

Jesus has been fasting for forty days and forty nights in this no-man's-land far beyond any city boundaries. Hunger is etched upon his face, high cheekbones starkly contrasting with the sunken hollows resulting from weeks without food.

The tempter is there. He sidles up to Jesus and whispers in a slithery voice, "If you are the Son of God, tell these stones to become bread."

Michael waits for the answer, hoping Jesus has the strength to endure his physical deprivation. Would he be able to resist the lure of bread, in spite of a painfully empty stomach?

Jesus answers, "It is written: 'Man does not live on bread alone, but on every word that comes from the mouth of God.'"

With a rush of wind, the Devil has taken Jesus. Michael searches the land for them, and his eyes rest upon the highest point of the temple. The Devil's voice is wheedling. "If you are the Son of God, ... throw yourself down. For it is written: 'He will command his angels concerning you, and they will lift you up in their hands, so that you will not strike your foot against a stone.'"

Michael knows the heart of Jesus, but still he wonders, *How strong is his will?*

Jesus answers, "It is also written: 'Do not put the Lord your God to the test.'"

Michael feels a moment's relief, and then the wind roars again. Next he sees the two figures on the top of a high mountain. The Devil is showing Jesus all the kingdoms of the world, and their splendor shines like gold in the midday sun.

"All this I will give you, ... if you will bow down and worship me."

Jesus didn't give in to satisfying a momentary need.

Michael hasn't even a moment to wonder if such power may corrupt the incorruptible. Jesus shouts, "Away from me, Satan! For it is written: 'Worship the Lord your God, and serve him only.'"

At that second, the Devil screams in frustration, then flees.

Michael takes to the skies, now free to bring his angelic aid to Jesus. Warmth and gratitude well up within him. The Son of God has shown great strength, standing up alone against the Prince of Darkness and winning a ferocious soul battle, the first of many more to come.

The temptation of Christ is deeply significant to us, his followers, who want to walk in his footsteps. Let's try to understand the events that occurred and what it meant for the sinless Son of God to have to endure a triple-test in the wilderness.

The first test involved Satan's appeal to the physical appetite. That's one that I identify with the most. Jesus had been in the desert, fasting for forty days. He had been led there by the Spirit of God, and he was following his Father's direction, obeying the Father's will. While Jesus had the power to turn the stones around him into bread, that was not the will of the Father. Jesus was to experience deprivation and hunger, and to satisfy that hunger would have been contrary to God's will.

What did Jesus do? He quoted Deuteronomy 8:3, as a reminder that man does not live on bread alone, but by God's Word. He stood strong, and didn't give in to satisfying a momentary need.

In the second test, Satan dangled the temptation of popularity and power. Here is a test that seems even more relevant in today's success-driven culture than it was in ancient times. Satan urged Jesus to throw himself off the temple roof and let the angels protect him. In other words, he tempted Jesus to make a huge show of his power and designation as Messiah.

He's a tricky one, that Satan, distorting God's Word to try and get his way. Here is one commentary on Satan's ploy:

> Satan may have thought if Jesus could quote Scripture to him, he could quote it too. However, he purposely did not quote Psalm 91:11–12 accurately. He left out an important phrase, "in all Your ways." According to the psalmist, a person is protected only when he is following the Lord's will. For Jesus to cast Himself down from the pinnacle of the temple in some dramatic display to

accommodate Himself to the people's thinking would not have been God's will. (*The Bible Knowledge Commentary, New Testament Edition*; John F. Walvoord and Roy B. Zuck, Victor Books)

> *The Lord . . . will give you the desires of your heart.*

Again, Jesus turned to the Word of God for his response, quoting from the book of Deuteronomy 6:16 that God should not be put to the test.

Satan's third test involved God's plan for Jesus. The Evil One tried to convince Jesus that there was an easier path to power and glory than the way of the cross God destined for his Son. All Jesus needed to do was bow down and worship Satan, and all the kingdoms of the world would belong to him. Of course, Jesus again responded from God's Word (see Deut. 6:13), that God alone should be worshipped and served. That ended the battle, and the angels rushed in to take care of Jesus' needs.

How does this relate to our own lives? Consider how Satan's temptations of people today often fall into the same three categories: fulfilling the physical appetite, meeting the desire for personal gain, and providing an easy path to power and glory. Sensual satisfaction, wealth and fame, and success are the hallmarks of our driven, contemporary society, and temptation often trumps the game of self-control.

Learning a Step at a Time

So how do we find self-control in a world that often rewards us with instant gratification? The answer is in turning it over to the Father who loves us and wants the very best for us.

Psalm 37:4–6 contains these words of hope and promise: "Delight yourself in the LORD and he will give you the desires of your heart. Commit your way to the LORD; trust in him and he will do this: He will make your righteousness shine like the dawn, the justice of your cause like the noonday sun."

If our desires become God's desires, we will find them fulfilled. Aligning our will with his allows this to happen naturally and without struggle. We don't have to force ourselves to "do the right thing" when his Spirit guides our steps. We will be able to live as people of the light, described here by the apostle Paul:

> You are all sons of the light and sons of the day. We do not belong to the night or to the darkness. So then, let us not be like others, who are asleep, but let us be alert and self-controlled. For those who sleep, sleep at night, and those who get drunk, get drunk at night. But since we belong to the day, let us be self-controlled, putting on faith and love as a breastplate, and the hope of salvation as a helmet. For God did not appoint us to suffer wrath but to receive salvation through our Lord Jesus Christ. He died for us so that, whether we are awake or asleep, we may live

together with him. Therefore encourage one
another and build each other up, just as in fact
you are doing. (1 Thess. 5:5–11)

In being one with Christ, you have the Spirit inside
you to help you follow in his footsteps. Not only that, we
have each other, members of the same body, to support
us as we seek to discover self-control, even in the most
tempting areas of life.

A friend of mine, a very self-disciplined person in
most ways, battled being overweight for many years. She
took the first step and joined Weight Watchers, through
which she lost more than two hundred pounds. The
proven program and the structure of meetings with like-
minded people gave my friend a great start. But lifelong
management required more. Eventually, she found the
key to inner healing through a recovery program that
relied on a higher power. Diet and exercise simply
weren't enough to maintain weight loss. The struggle for
self-control went straight to the soul's deepest levels.

Self-control in Action

As we've worked together to understand the fruit of the
Spirit as described in Galatians 5:22–23, we have con-
sidered many good examples of love, joy, peace,
patience, kindness, goodness, faithfulness, gentleness,
and self-control. As inspiring as good examples can be,

sometimes much more may be learned by studying a bad example.

How would you like it if your life stood forever as a bad example? How would you feel if one instance of lack of self-control changed the history of an entire race and your terrible decision was recorded and retained in the world's best-selling book for everyone to see? How would you like to have been Esau, the guy whose food craving led to a second-place finish in the race of his life?

We find his story in Genesis 25—27. Esau was the twin brother of Jacob, and both were the children of Isaac and Rebekah. From the very beginning, these brothers fought for space and dominance: "The babies jostled each other within [Rebekah], and she said, 'Why is this happening to me?' So she went to inquire of the LORD.

"The LORD said to her, 'Two nations are in your womb, and two peoples from within you will be separated; one people will be stronger than the other, and the older will serve the younger'" (Gen. 25:22–23).

When the boys were born, they were clearly fraternal twins. Esau popped out first. His skin was red-tinged and he was born hairy, while Jacob was right behind him, grabbing onto his brother's heel. (The name Jacob was actually a pun on the Hebrew word for *grasp*, while Esau's name came from the word for *red*.)

As the two brothers grew up, their differences became even more apparent. Esau became a skillful hunter who loved the great outdoors, while quiet Jacob spent time among the tents, helping his mother and learning to be a really good cook. Their father, age sixty when they were born, grew to love Esau better, because the hunter was able to keep his elderly father supplied with tasty wild game.

Rebekah favored her smooth-skinned boy, Jacob. She knew he was at a disadvantage because he'd been born second, and as the younger brother he lacked the birthright, which went to only-moments-older Esau. According to ancient custom, the birthright involved getting a greater share of the family inheritance and receiving the privileges and responsibilities of family leadership. Only a rash fool would give up such a position of prestige.

One day Esau came back from a lengthy hunting trip and smelled the lentil stew simmering in a pot tended by Jacob. He had been out all day in the open country with little to eat. Now he felt starved, and lentil stew was his favorite meal. The scent of it nearly drove him crazy.

"Quick," he said to Jacob, "let me have some of that red stew! I'm famished!"

Jacob looked at his brother steadily. "First sell me your birthright."

"Look, I am about to die," Esau said. "What good is the birthright to me?"

But Jacob said, "Swear to me first."

So Esau swore an oath to his brother, selling his birthright for a pot of stew and a hunk of bread. He devoured the meal, patted his full belly, and went on his way, giving no thought to the turmoil his sudden decision would create in the future.

Eventually Jacob would get to become the family leader, unfairly and craftily stealing his father's blessing from Esau in another swift move. A moment of instant gratification finally led to the foundation of the nation of Israel, which would take prominence over Esau's descendants, the Edomites, and form the basis for a grudge that could never be fully healed.

While Esau is a model for failed self-control, Jacob's story reveals a fairly good ability to control his passions. Later in his life, on the run and in hiding from his twin brother who, for good reasons, wanted to kill him, Jacob went to work for his uncle Laban. There he fell in love with Laban's daughter, a beautiful shepherdess named Rachel. He was so much in love that he agreed to Laban's terms: seven years of free labor in return for Rachel's hand in marriage.

The long years went by and Jacob patiently waited for his bride. But on the wedding night, Laban pulled a switch and substituted Rachel's older sister Leah. When Jacob figured it out (remember, it could be pretty dark out there in the desert), it was the morning of the next day and too late to undo the marriage. Laban said Jacob would have to finish out the bridal week with Leah, keep her as a wife, and then he could marry Rachel. Of course, in exchange, he'd have to work the next seven years for his dear uncle Laban.

I think Jacob showed remarkable self-control, not only for working a total of fourteen years to have the woman he loved, but also for not killing his tricky uncle.

Naturally life wasn't all that easy with two sisters as rival wives, but Jacob's many offspring included Joseph (of the famed coat of many colors), who eventually became a leader in Egypt and a patriarch of God's people. Jacob's self-control ultimately grew out of his relationship with God and his willingness to follow the path God set before him.

In the end, impatience proved a costly mistake for Esau, but self-control paid off for Jacob and his family.

Gardener's Tools for Life

In what areas do you battle for self-control? Make a list in your journal. It might involve physical addictions and habits such as overeating, anorexia and bulimia, or alcoholism. Perhaps your battles include such emotional issues as anger management or depression. Or you want to incorporate healthy spiritual habits such as Bible study and regular prayer time, but you find yourself failing to be consistent. Are more of your self-control issues relational? Do you struggle with gossip or criticism or a spirit of unforgiveness? Spend time doing a self-inventory before you write down your list.

After you have identified core areas to improve in

your life, spend time in prayer submitting them to God, asking the Holy Spirit to take control of each one.

In Proverbs 25:28 we read, "Like a city whose walls are broken down is a man who lacks self-control." When a city's walls are broken down, it is susceptible to attack. Think about the results in your life when the walls of self-control break down. Write about the consequences in your journal.

If you have been battling alone in an area where you lack self-control, consider getting help from a support group related to your church or located in your region. It can be difficult, but finding out you're not alone in your journey can open a door to healing.

Create a physical symbol that reminds you to submit a particular problem area to God. It could be as simple as a drawing of a donut with a circle around it and a line through it! It could be a fresh flower that you keep in a vase, to remind you of the beauty of growing stronger in your life. Whatever you devise, make sure you can take a look at this symbol when you are tempted, then be reminded that you can do all things through Christ who strengthens you.

Read these words to the wise from King Solomon, a great king of Israel who had little patience for those who lacked self-control. Of course, he seemed to lack control where women were concerned, but everybody has a blind spot, right? Enjoy the lively language and picture these colorful images from Proverbs 6:6–11 in your imagination. Then ask yourself if "bandits" have stolen anything from your life as you have been sleeping.

> Go to the ant, you sluggard;
>   consider its ways and be wise!
> It has no commander,
>   no overseer or ruler,
> yet it stores its provisions in summer
>   and gathers its food at harvest.
> How long will you lie there, you sluggard?
>   When will you get up from your sleep?
> A little sleep, a little slumber,
>   a little folding of the hands to rest—
> and poverty will come on you like a bandit
>   and scarcity like an armed man.

Copy the following scripture passages into your journal and meditate on them in the week to come.

> I do not run like a man running aimlessly; I do not fight like a man beating the air. No, I beat my body and make it my slave so that after I have preached to others, I myself will not be disqualified for the prize. (1 Cor. 9:26–27)

(The apostle Paul compares his spiritual goals to the physical drive of athletes in training: No pain, no gain!)

> Teach the older men to be temperate, worthy of respect, self-controlled, and sound in faith, in love and in endurance.
>   Likewise, teach the older women to be reverent in the way they live, not to be slanderers or addicted to much wine, but to teach what is good. Then they can train the younger women to love

their husbands and children, to be self-controlled and pure, to be busy at home, to be kind, and to be subject to their husbands, so that no one will malign the word of God. (Titus 2:2–5)

(The apostle Paul instructs the young leader Titus about how to teach church members to act in a godly manner.)

The wisdom that comes from heaven is first of all pure; then peace-loving, considerate, submissive, full of mercy and good fruit, impartial and sincere....

Submit yourselves, then, to God. Resist the devil, and he will flee from you. Come near to God and he will come near to you. (James 3:17; 4:7–8)

Conclusion

A Fruitful Life

It was an ordinary evening, just another summer kids' baseball game, when the line between life and death split time as sharply as a lightning bolt divides the night sky.

I'd been enjoying the peaceful beauty and slow pace of the game. Jonathan's team even inspired me to write this in my journal: "I love to see these thirteen-year-old boys in their baseball uniforms. They look so tidy—tucked-in and clean—compared to their ordinary baggy-pants-and-big-shirt disarray. At an age where chaos still prevails in areas of hygiene, it's comforting to see how order can be imposed, if only for the two-hour length of a Parks and Rec baseball game."

The game was drawing to a close. Jonathan was having his best game ever, five hits for five times at bat. All seemed calm and happy. But this game would never be finished.

When a referee made a questionable call, our assistant coach, Dennis, grimaced in annoyance. His wife, Mary—laughing loud and hard at her husband's obvious irritation—turned to look up and back toward the rest of us on the bleachers. Suddenly, her face went blank, her eyes closed, and she fell backward.

People quickly realized Mary was in trouble. Somebody called 911. Somebody started to perform CPR. It felt like forever, but ten minutes later a fire truck arrived. As the EMTs worked to stabilize Mary, a neighbor hugged her son and hustled him away from the sight. The boys and coach gathered in the infield, quiet, with anxious faces.

I watched as if paralyzed, wanting to help, but able to do nothing but pray. When the boys at last came in from the field, I went to my son and tried to reassure him, but I was not at all sure that Mary would be all right.

The sky darkened and the night grew colder. An ambulance came, and the paramedics carried Mary on a stretcher to it, and it left for the hospital, siren on, lights flashing. Other team parents drove coach Dennis, who seemed to be in shock, and his son to the hospital.

We left the park in darkness, but before we drove away, the sunset lit the sky like a fire struck by a match spark. The mountains stood in their eternal profile against the orange clouds. It looked like a bonfire in heaven.

The next day I learned that Mary died in the night. An aneurysm rushed her away from friends and family in the middle of a moment, in the midst of life and laughter.

Though I didn't know the forty-eight-year-old mother of three very well, I felt compelled to attend her funeral service. The large church was packed.

A woman close to my age stood to speak. "Mary was my best friend," she said. "She was your best friend too."

Some day each of us will leave behind a legacy.

The woman went on to describe Mary and told about her lifetime of loving and giving. The sixth of ten children, Mary had lived all her life in our town, worked in the family business, and made herself the heart of her large, close family. Mary's job was to hold the babies and cut the cake at every celebration, they said.

Stories about Mary and the suddenness of her loss touched me deeply as I wondered what it would be like if I was snatched from this earth as quickly as she was. Like Mary, I'm in the middle of a very busy, full life. Am I making the most of it for those around me?

These words from a booklet distributed at a funeral picturing Mary's radiantly smiling face describe a woman whose life bore fruit in many ways. Her example stands as a testimony of the power of the Spirit to change us into reflections of Jesus. As fruit is born in our lives, it will inevitably plant seeds in the lives of our family and friends.

> Mary lived life at double speed—perhaps, unconsciously, she was driven by a deep and private sense of urgency that she had to fit ninety years into forty-eight. Yet even in the most hectic and chaotic schedule, she had a quiet passion for her family. She never ceased to wonder at the miracle of her children, and she never stopped thanking God for Dennis and his love for her and the kids.
>
> Each of her children is so very like her: Teresa reflects her spirited energy, intelligence, stubborn focus, and depth of decency; Curtis has her courage, sensitivity, and a deep awareness of others before himself; Lucas has her smile, her kindness, her powerful need to have everyone together. Above all, each has her love of family. They were taught by Mary, as she was taught by her parents, that the most important thing in our human lives is simply to love each other.
>
> Mary sets the gold standard for loving. She teaches us today that if we fill our lives with love, there is no room in our hearts for hate.
>
> Mary had so much love to give because she kept giving it away. Let us try to do the same.

Love, joy, peace, patience, kindness, goodness, faithfulness, gentleness, self-control. Mary's life bore the fruit of the Spirit, even though it was cut far too short. And that fruit will produce seeds in the lives of her family members and friends, which will blossom into eternity.

May we each look to the present and seek to bear fruit in these day-to-day moments. May we be reminded that some day each of us will leave behind a legacy for those who knew us. I pray your legacy will be as sweet and nourishing as a bowl of fresh fruit, and last for generations to come.

Readers' Guide

*for Personal Reflection
or Group Discussion*

Readers' Guide

*A*re you somebody who is so taxed and tired that you don't even have the energy to write a to-do list, let alone take on the very first task? The good news is that a journey through the nine characteristics that comprise the fruit of the Spirit is not a type of spiritual must-do list at all. Instead it's a treasure that will feed your soul and energize you in new ways. Learning to lean on the One who made us, enables each of us to grow in the reflection of Jesus Christ.

As you walk through these pages, please understand that the fruit of the Spirit—love, joy, peace, patience, kindness, goodness, faithfulness, gentleness, self-control—offers a better life for you and those you love. And it's much more about yielding than working hard and producing a bumper crop.

The purpose of this study guide, and the book as a whole, is to help you learn the habit of grace. Too many Christian women know the law well and are burning out because of the emphasis on doing everything perfectly under their own power. To have something to give spiritually, one must first receive God's grace in your life and fully own it. I trust this study will help you do that.

The questions that follow have been designed for use by individuals or groups. Use this guide during your personal devotions, with a prayer partner, in a Bible study group, or a Sunday school class. However you utilize this study, may you gain a fuller and deeper understanding of what it means to live a life that reflects the fruit of the Spirit in every way.

Introduction

1. How closely do you identify with Miss Betty? Are you living a balanced life today?

2. If your life is out of balance and you could imagine it as a scale, what areas would be in the heavily weighted side of the scale? Which areas are in the lighter side?

3. Have you ever done a study of the fruit of the Spirit before? If so, what did you take away from it? If not, what are your expectations? Why did you want to take on this study?

4. Look at the list of characteristics defined by the fruit of the Spirit in Galatians 5:22–23: love, joy, peace, patience, kindness, goodness, faithfulness, gentleness, and self-control. Which one seems to come the most easily to you? Which is your biggest challenge?

5. As you embark on this study, pause for a few quiet moments and ask God to lead it for you. Honestly seek a life-changing journey toward wholeness and a spirit that will grow more intimately connected with the True Vine.

Chapter 1:
The Fruit of the Spirit Is ... Love

1. Identify a person who has modeled love in your life.

2. What aspect of that person's love meant the most to you personally?

3. Mother Teresa said that anyone may gather the fruit of love through meditation, a spirit of prayer and sacrifice, and an intense inner life. What obstacles in your modern life hinder the gathering of those tools?

4. How did Jesus show love to his disciples? Why did Peter respond the way he did?

5. In what way do you need to have Jesus minister to you today? What, if anything, stands in the way?

6. Reread 1 John 3:1, 11, 18–24. What does it mean, in practical terms, to "not love with words or tongue but with actions and in truth"?

Chapter 2:
The Fruit of the Spirit Is ... Joy

1. What is usually the happiest day of the year for you? What was the happiest day of the last year? Why was it the most joyful?

2. What makes joy a hybrid fruit?

3. Describe a bittersweet experience in your own life. What was the most bitter part? The sweetest?

4. What in your life most consistently contrives to steal your joy?

5. Who do you know who exemplifies contagious joy? What aspect of this person's spirit makes this so?

6. Why was the baptism of Jesus a joyful occasion?

7. What are some traditional ways you express your praise to God? Describe some less conventional means of praising him. What is the connection between joy and praise?

Chapter 3:
The Fruit of the Spirit Is ... Peace

1. On a scale of one to ten (one being low, ten being high), how peaceful is your life?

2. Describe an oasis of peace in your life, if one exists. Contrast it to any specific storms in your life today.

3. Sara saw a butterfly during a time of worry, and it became a symbol of peace and God's care. If you could choose a symbol to remind you to seek peace, what would it be?

4. Why did Jesus commend Mary in the account retold in this chapter? Did you identify more with Mary or with Martha? Why?

5. How do you spend time at the feet of Jesus? What would you change?

6. What challenges are you facing today that you want to place into God's hands?

7. Can you honestly say, as in the hymn, that "it is well with my soul"? If not, what steps might help you move closer to that declaration?

Chapter 4:
The Fruit of the Spirit Is ... Patience

1. Would you describe yourself as a patient person? Why or why not?

2. Think back over the past three weeks. What has tested your patience most severely?

3. Do you think it was difficult for Jesus to be patient with the children in the story retold in this chapter? Why or why not? What about the disciples?

4. What in your life do you fear might cause God to lose patience with you? Do you believe his patience is eternal? Why or why not?

5. How can we develop the humility that leads to a spirit of patience?

6. Do you know anyone with a servant's heart? How might you encourage that person today?

7. In Psalm 27:13 we read, "I am still confident of this: I will see the goodness of the LORD in the land of the living." Do you believe your own life reflects this confident attitude? Why or why not?

Chapter 5:
The Fruit of the Spirit Is ... Kindness

1. What's the kindest thing anyone has ever done for you? How did it make you feel?

2. What was most significant about the story of the woman pouring perfume on Jesus' feet? What would be a modern-day equivalent of this woman's sacrificial act?

3. How are kindness and grace intertwined?

4. What is the opposite of kindness? Describe an example you have witnessed or read about in the recent past. What was the outcome?

5. Proverbs 14:31 states, "Whoever is kind to the needy honors God." Why do you think this is true?

6. What is the relationship between kindness and forgiveness?

Chapter 6:
The Fruit of the Spirit Is ... Goodness

1. Do you believe there are more good people than evil people in the world today? Why or why not?

2. Describe a good person in your life. What is it about that person that demonstrates his or her goodness?

3. Why was it so good of Jesus to interact with the woman at the well? What changed in the woman's life as a result of her encounter with Jesus?

4. Describe a time you took a risk to do something good. Was it difficult or easy? Why?

5. Have you ever tried to do something good and it backfired? What happened? How did you feel about it?

6. In what way does Jesus fulfill the role of Good Shepherd in your life?

Chapter 7:
The Fruit of the Spirit Is ... Faithfulness

1. What is something you've had to do faithfully? How long did you persevere?

2. Name some tasks you perform daily or regularly. What are the consequences of neglecting those tasks?

3. How did Jesus demonstrate faithfulness in relation to his friends Mary, Martha, and Lazarus?

4. In what way has the Lord been faithful to you? How have you responded to his faithfulness?

5. What are your best excuses employed for avoiding tasks that require faithfulness? How legitimate are those excuses?

6. Describe someone who has been an example of faithfulness in your life. What obstacles did that person have to overcome in order to make a difference?

7. How are faithfulness, kindness, and goodness similar? How are they different?

Chapter 8:
The Fruit of the Spirit Is ... Gentleness

1. Take out crayons or colored pencils and draw a picture representing gentleness. What colors did you use? Why does it express gentleness to you?

2. Why is strength a hidden aspect of gentleness?

3. How did Jesus exemplify gentleness combined with strength? In what ways does he withhold his strength when dealing with us?

4. In the hymn "Lead, Kindly Light," lyricist John Newman asks the Lord to lead us through the dark and over difficult ground, until the night is gone. In what way does God lead you through your most difficult times? How is that an example of grace?

5. How is Jesus a "Soul Whisperer" in your life? When do you find it hard to be gentle? How can Jesus make a difference during those periods of your life?

6. Take time to pray for gentleness. Spend some quiet moments mentally picturing a concrete symbol of gentleness, perhaps the one you drew. Ask the Lord to bring that to reality in your heart. Submit to changes that may be required to open the door to a gentle spirit.

Chapter 9:
The Fruit of the Spirit Is ... Self-control

1. Where and when do you find it hardest to demonstrate self-control? Which areas of your life represent the battleground?

2. When have you experienced victories of self-control? To what do you attribute those successes?

3. What weapons did Jesus employ in his battle against temptation? How are those weapons available to us?

4. If your life could be represented by a tree, a shrub, or even a strawberry patch, how much pruning would be required? What is required for the pruning to be successful?

5. What does it mean to "delight yourself in the LORD" (Ps. 37:4)? What specific steps will lead to a state of delighting yourself in the Lord? What changes in your life will take you further along your journey toward self-control and obtaining the desires of your heart?

Conclusion:
A Fruitful Life

1. In the conclusion, the funeral of a woman whose life ended suddenly served as a testimony to the fruit of the Spirit she exhibited to many. What would you hope would be said about you, if that were your funeral service?

2. Do you have a joyful expectation of eternity? Why or why not?

3. What, for you, will be the key to experience the blessing of a more fruitful life today?

Bibliography

Brown, Dale and Dorothy. 2005. Kind-hearted patron honored couple with dinner. Colorado Springs *Gazette*, June 15.

Morton, Jane Ambrose. *Cowboy Poetry: Turning to Face the Wind*. Phoenix, AZ: Cowboy Miner Productions, 2004. The poem "The Apricot Tree" is used by permission.

Muggeridge, Malcolm. *Something Beautiful for God*. San Francisco: HarperSanFrancisco, 1986.

The Quest Study Bible. Grand Rapids, MI: Zondervan, 1994.

Ryrie, Charles. *Basic Theology*. Wheaton, IL: Victor, 1986.

Simons, Janet. 1995. Kid anecdotes show mothers are just human. *Rocky Mountain News,* July 18, 3D.

Vogrin, Bill. 2005. Fire brings neighbors, new friends together. Colorado Springs *Gazette,* June 13, metro section.

Walvoord, John F., and Roy B. Zuck. *The Bible Knowledge Commentary.* Wheaton, IL: Victor, 1983.

White, John. *The Fight.* Downers Grove, IL: InterVarsity Press, 1976.

Additional copies of *BLOOM BEFORE YOU'RE PLANTED*
and other Life Journey titles are available
wherever good books are sold.

If you have enjoyed this book,
or if it has had an impact on your life,
we would like to hear from you.

Please contact us at:

LIFE JOURNEY BOOKS
Cook Communications Ministries, Dept. 201
4050 Lee Vance View
Colorado Springs, CO 80918

Or visit our Web site:
www.cookministries.com

LIFE JOURNEY®
Bringing Home the Message for Life